Praise for *Marinovich*

"A rocket ride to football stardom in the high times of LA, Todd's story will blow you away. *Marinovich* pulls you into the real-life dreams and nightmares that accompany fame, and you will emerge with a greater appreciation of one of the most misunderstood football players of a generation."

—Troy Polamalu, Pro Football Hall of Famer

"Todd is an artist and an amazing football player who exceeded the expectations surrounding him on the field. He became the number one high school football player in the nation, led USC to a Rose Bowl win as a freshman, and joined an NFL team when he was barely a man...but at what cost? *Marinovich* will shock you with its mind-bending insights."

—Marcus Allen, Pro Football Hall of Famer
and former Raiders Running Back

"Todd's story is both tragic and inspirational. As a player and coach, I never stopped hoping the world would see and know the depth and breadth of his talents. He's deserving of our love and compassion for never giving up on his journey to heal."

—Fred Biletnikoff, Pro Football Hall of Famer
and former Raiders Coach

"A revealing read from start to finish, Todd is profoundly honest about his life and his struggles. If you follow football and the players behind the masks, this is a must-read."

—Tim Brown, Pro Football Hall of Famer and former Raiders Wide Receiver

"There is no lack of sports books on shelves, but there are few that offer *Marinovich*'s insights about childhood trauma and elite athletics with brutal honesty and humility forged by more than 35 years of addiction and self-discovery."

—Terry Robiskie, former NFL Coach

"Todd Marinovich rightfully evokes controversy with a name attached to provocative headlines. From his unconventional upbringing, rise to USC, and time in the NFL, Todd doesn't hold back in *Marinovich*."

—Pat Harlow, USC Teammate and former NFL Offensive Tackle

"A gripping and brutally honest story of incredible highs and bottomless lows, told with integrity from the man who lived it all. Todd Marinovich squandered what should have been a legendary football career, but, ultimately, his willingness to share the details of his life journey will prove all the more important and lasting."

—Jeff Pearlman, *New York Times* Bestselling Author

MARINOVICH

Also by Lizzy Wright

Aggressively Human: Discovering Humanity in the NFL, Reality TV, and Life (with Steve Wright)

MARINOVICH

Outside the Lines in Football, Art, and Addiction

TODD MARINOVICH
with Lizzy Wright

Matt Holt Books
An Imprint of BenBella Books, Inc.
Dallas, TX

Marinovich copyright © 2025 by Todd Marinovich with Lizzy Wright

All rights reserved. Except in the case of brief quotations embodied in critical articles or reviews, no part of this book may be used or reproduced, stored, transmitted, or used in any manner whatsoever, including for training artificial intelligence (AI) technologies or for automated text and data mining, without prior written permission from the publisher.

Photographs furnished by USC Athletics and Raiders Football Club, LLC

Matt Holt is an imprint of BenBella Books, Inc.
8080 N. Central Expressway
Suite 1700
Dallas, TX 75206
benbellabooks.com
Send feedback to feedback@benbellabooks.com

BenBella and *Matt Holt* are federally registered trademarks.

Printed in the United States of America
10 9 8 7 6 5 4 3 2 1

Library of Congress Control Number: 2025001598
ISBN 9781637747100 (hardcover)
ISBN 9781637747117 (electronic)

Editing by Lydia Choi
Copyediting by Jennifer Greenstein
Proofreading by Sarah Vostok and Ashley Casteel
Text design and composition by Jordan Koluch
Cover design by Brigid Pearson
Printed by Sheridan MI

**Special discounts for bulk sales are available.
Please contact bulkorders@benbellabooks.com.**

For those brave enough to live their truth

Contents

Prologue   xv

Chapter One: **Tapped Out**   1
Chapter Two: **Flirting with the Third Rail**   3
Chapter Three: **Bred to Be?**   29
Chapter Four: **A Bloody Spiral**   47
Chapter Five: **Marijuana-vich**   67
Chapter Six: **High Functioning or Functioning High?**
    My USC Days   85
Chapter Seven: **The Fucking Sun Bowl?**   111
Chapter Eight: **A Renegade Gone Awry**   121
Chapter Nine: **A Headshot or a Mug Shot?**
    The Grip of Addiction   167
Chapter Ten: **Art and Recovery**   191
Chapter Eleven: **Full Circle**   209

Epilogue: Hard-Won Wisdom   217
Acknowledgments   219

In a society that profits from your self-doubt, liking yourself is a rebellious act.

—Caroline Caldwell

This book is an act of self-love after decades of self-defiance.

While I have re-created some conversations from my memories, the essence of my story, and the feelings and emotions evoked, are accurate representations of what actually happened. To protect the privacy of some individuals, I purposefully changed select names and identifying details. Any resemblance between a fictionalized name and a real person is strictly coincidental. In passages containing dialogue, I have used quotation marks to represent the speaker's words as accurately as possible and to convey the intended meaning of what was said. Also, consider this fair warning: the book contains language that may be offensive to some readers, but it is included to reflect what was said and done before movements that have evolved the collective consciousness. No disrespect is intended.

Prologue

"If you could be anyone in Los Angeles, who would you be?"

It wasn't a complicated poll—classic fodder for *The Mark & Brian Show*. I loved these radio personalities, rarely missing an episode on my way to work.

The dash clock showed 7:45 AM. I was supposed to be on the training table getting my ankles taped. Bring on the late fine. I wouldn't be satisfied with a cliff-hanger. As I rounded the last corner to enter the Raiders training camp facility, Brian teed up the results.

The first choice was obvious: Magic Johnson. He was synonymous with Los Angeles. Even his HIV diagnosis had barely tarnished his public image.

The second pick nearly caused me to crash my ride.

"Todd Marinovich." Out of all the athletes, musicians, actors, and celebrities in Los Angeles, the audience chose me—pure insanity.

There's no way anybody would want my life if they knew what it was really like.

Two hours later, the Raiders released me.

So much for the fairy tale.

———

Buckle up. This isn't about football, although that's where it starts and ends. It's a painful love story on a dark, twisted path toward self-acceptance. I'm the sum of a million different decisions. I own them all. Some come with heavy regret and a conveyor belt of baggage, while others usher in redemption with hidden watersheds of joy.

No one pushed me into football, least of all my dad, Marv. I chose it. Any suggestions to the contrary were lies offered freely by the media to manufacture a Greek tragedy. Worse yet, I peddled similar falsehoods in my darker moments to appease the relentless badgers. Ironically, I was so skilled at lying that everyone, including me, believed them. My deceit knew no bounds: from diet to football and Marv, but most often, my sobriety. I said what others wanted to hear or what might make my life easier at the moment, objective truth be damned.

Marv was a thorny scapegoat, as he'd delivered the genes and created the environment offering addiction fertile ground. He could be a ruthless tyrant obsessed with perfection, but ultimately, his criticism was child's play. The most damaging voice came from within. At the height of addiction, I needed drugs to silence my mind as much as others require air. The relentless quest turned my life into material for nightmares. I didn't know it was possible to inflict so much harm on my death march.

A harsh reality accompanied addiction: There wasn't a cure. The insidious nature of my illness meant that it always loomed just out of view. It awaited complacency to return with an unmatched fervor. So my wellness was contingent upon discipline and hard work—two things I knew well, introduced in the crib under Marv's watchful eye. This early primer set the stage for my demise, yet also my eventual salvation: a nuance lost on many commentators and armchair quarterbacks.

Decades later, I finally owned my addictive personality. But it was nearly too late. It wasn't easy to accept that my most fundamental flaw was both a tremendous blessing and a horrible curse, but it was my reality. I saw the contradiction as clear as daylight. Without the zeal accompanying obsession, who knows if I would've succeeded in football? Someone else could have been the first college sophomore in history to declare for the NFL draft. Yet, on the flip side, there wouldn't have been a soul-crushing dozen arrests, five incarcerations, and over seven trips to rehab.

I've been many things in life: a son, athlete, artist, addict, husband, father, and, most importantly, survivor. I'll never stop fighting like hell to stay well enough for myself and those I love. While we may never meet, that includes you.

Chapter One

Tapped Out

December 1, 2002.

The syringe is too dull to pierce my jugular.

There are no virgins left on my body; every vein has been abused to silence the agony. I am desperate for a reprieve, but it will be short-lived before the storm returns, bearing down with unrelenting sheets of hurt, doubt, and self-loathing. Each time I'm hopeful the heroin will permanently silence this raging tempest, but I'm never so lucky.

The smell of death lingers in the fetid air. I don't want to die, yet this isn't living.

As I sharpen the large-gauge needle with a file, the scraping metals sound as wretched as I feel. It's an out-of-body ache as I look down on an unrecognizable man. My skin hangs loosely from my weak bones. I'm a shell of a person, emaciated and propped up against a wall, alone in a vacant warehouse in East Los Angeles. I rise to shatter the mirror because I'm afraid of what I will see.

I forgo a tourniquet. It feels like a noose around my neck and a terrible way to die. But I need to expose the entry point for relief. I take a deep inhale as I've done a million times before. I'm not duck-diving a wave in the surf, though; I'm risking my life for a high. *Is this my fatal last breath?* It doesn't matter; it's not a choice. If I don't shove the needle into this swollen vein, the agony of withdrawal will become all-consuming.

I brace myself against a filthy sink, leaning in as my lungs scream for air. My body fights for its life as the lights dim. I'm about to go dark, so I thrust the needle into my neck. The skin pops, and I wait. As my eyes flutter, I weave in and out of consciousness. My synapses slow to a crawl as I imagine blood mushrooming into the syringe to signal blissful contact. The euphoric warmth surges faster than a rising tide throughout my body. Extracting the weapon from my left hand, I apply pressure on the puncture point. It's like covering a garden hose with my thumb as the blood wants out to expose the carnage.

This can't be me, but it is.

It takes decades to process everything that led me to this moment. Heroin is both a god and a devil suspended in a syringe of fleeting bliss. But hasn't that been true of everything in my life, including the ephemeral nature of football and fame?

Chapter Two

Flirting with the Third Rail

I didn't end up in a warehouse after just one bender. Although the universe offered warnings, not even the humiliation of an arrest altered my trajectory. I watched the 1990 American Football Conference (AFC) championship game between the bars of a holding cell. No fucking joke. How did I get there? I asked the same question many times that day.

After a disastrous sideline fight with University of Southern California (USC) coach Larry Smith at the Sun Bowl my sophomore year, I needed to hang up my Trojan helmet. It was time to go for the pros. I wasn't quite ready to leave college football and my teammates. But ESPN caught the nasty exchange with my dogmatic coach, and any subpar lip reader could see me announce, "I'm outta here." Those three words set the gears in motion. By that evening, *SportsCenter* had aired the love spat, and it hit the wire, spreading verbal vomit.

A month later, I blew off steam with buddies in Newport Beach, California. It was the perfect antidote to lingering tension from the bowl game. We barhopped through the daytime party scene and continued deep into the night. At 4 AM, the fun meter was stuck on high with the volume to match. I was so close to home—a mere twenty yards from my family's clapboard beach house. Yet I was a million miles away, lost in my stupor, when snared by the boys in blue.

Were we out of control? Nah. Loud as hell? Most definitely. At 4:15 AM, our substance-induced confidence turned us into walking megaphones, practically beckoning the police to our location. The beat cops rolled up fast. I didn't have time to hide the goods—the gram of cocaine burning a hole in my left pocket. It was a bona fide code red, cracking the party atmosphere with the force of a sledgehammer.

The cops started with my buddies. This gave me time to pray for a graze-n-go pat down before my turn. But feeling my anxiety spike in anticipation, I made an unfortunate game-time decision. I casually eased a hand into my pocket to palm the seeds of my demise. Grabbing the baggie, I slid it down my backside to hide between my cheeks like a drug mule. One of the cops caught the motion out of the corner of his eye as I completed the move. He dropped me to the ground faster than an outside linebacker.

"Okay, fucking Robo Quarterback, I saw that shit," he snarled, reluctantly shoving his hand down the back of my jeans and aggressively parting my cheeks. "Jesus Christ, look what you made me do, you asshole." The beefy young cop, maybe three years my senior and still peppered with cystic acne, held up the ratty baggie trophy between two fingers.

In shock after getting waylaid, I twisted my neck off the filthy pavement to examine his facial features for signs of familiarity. There had to be some high school overlap. Given his tone and demeanor, we must've played for rival schools. *Football, basketball, or baseball?* With the number of teams and games that littered my childhood, the possibilities were endless. But whatever sport we had in common, that's where our similarities ended. I'd veered left, and this kid had taken a hard right in life, coloring inside the lines.

I was cuffed, read my Miranda rights, and handled as a fugitive while the cops shooed off my crew. With my anxiety redlining, they crammed me into the back of a squad car as if I were a danger to society. I wasn't a criminal; I just needed to escape. *How could I explain in a way that they'd understand?* Hauling me in would make more sense if I'd hurt someone other than myself. It struck me then, and still does today, that we criminalize addicts when their only truly harmful crime is usually self-inflicted. But it was no time to resist arrest. The headlines would be bad enough already.

On the ride to the Newport Beach City Jail, I envisioned the arches of Marv's bushy eyebrows when he received the news. Marv would lose his shit. So much was on the line as I declared for the NFL draft. This was the last, no, far beyond the last, thing I needed. My professional career could end before it even launched. I'd be the player that never was, Marv's crowning achievement gone awry. All the years of sacrifice, training, sweat equity, and tears would be for nothing. That little baggie that eased my pain also caused an incalculable number of problems.

I was booked on one count of cocaine possession, my first arrest of many to follow. Then they moved me to a holding cell. My mind swirled, and the pit in my stomach grew in lockstep with my increasing sobriety. The clanking of the cell triggered feelings of entrapment. The wild animal in me wanted out. I desperately needed a distraction. I reflexively turned in response to a ref's whistle, a distant sound so familiar to me that it was like a nursery rhyme. There had to be a football game on. Sure enough, I looked up out of my misery at a distant TV screen flashing with the silver and black that dominated my childhood. The Los Angeles Raiders, Marv's old team when they were in Oakland, were knee-deep in a shitstorm, embarrassed by the Buffalo Bills. I stood transfixed as Jim Kelly fumbled a snap, only to have it bounce back into his hands before throwing a touchdown to James Lofton without breaking stride. No matter what the Raiders did, it wasn't their day. I knew *exactly* how they felt.

I couldn't hear much other than the whistle, but that was fine. I always listened to games on mute anyway. I didn't need someone to fill in the gaps. I wanted to get a closer look at the action, though. With a billboard-shaped backside, the duty guard blocked much of my view. After some maneuvering on the unforgiving cement, I found a sliver of the screen. I welded my cheekbones into the steel bars to watch the players who, unbeknownst to me, would be my future teammates.

The game kept my mind off my circumstances temporarily. But as the matchup concluded, the magnitude of my situation returned with the force of a Category 4 hurricane. I had a few hours of wicked, soul-slicing self-talk in my temporary quarters. My self-loathing, usually a steady six, hit an eleven out of ten. I paced, mumbled under my breath, and stared into the abyss, desperate to thaw time.

I wondered who would bail me out. *Please let it be anyone but Marv.* I prayed for the first time since Catholic school. With more gusto the second time: *Anyone but Marv.* I didn't realize the shortsightedness of these pleas until moments later. A recognizable voice, as deep as the ocean, pulled me from my angst-ridden appeal. I detected a familiar aftershave overtaking the stench of unwashed misfits that consumed the lockup. Twisting my neck, I discovered my savior. I locked eyes with Papa, the former police chief of Huntington Park. He was here to pick up his grandson. *Dear God.*

He proudly wore a USC booster jacket over his full belly and boxy frame as he occupied the space beyond the bars. While the duty guard fumbled with his keys, Papa gave me more than a message with his eyes. It was not of anger but of complete and utter despair. This was worse than Marv because it appealed to my heart. I bit my lip and looked down while completing my out-processing. Then we left the clink, two wordless carrottops making their way to the vacant lot. Still speechless, we idled in his Cadillac until he broke through the tension.

"I had to put up the beach house to get you out of there," he said, his voice thick and gentle as he slipped the car into gear.

"I'm sorry, Papa, it won't happen again." I honestly believed it, but it was a temporary truth.

The silence on the ride home to the family beach house was worse than a tense family dinner. It wasn't more than ten miles from the city jail, but that short jaunt took half an hour on a good day in Southern California. The gridlocked 405 Freeway moved slower than a line at Disneyland. I stared at the sea of cars, unable to convert thoughts into words.

Finally, we pulled into the garage. Papa left me alone in the car as I sat, unblinking, in my internal house of pain. *What would I say to Mom?* She knew everything: my struggle with the pressure, the inescapable fame, and the desire to be anyone but Todd Marinovich. She understood it all, except that drugs were the only relief. I could taste the words I was supposed to say but would not: "never again."

I tiptoed through the entryway. Mom paced like a cat in a cage, her usually perfect brown coif in a disheveled knot and her eyes still swollen from a night of worry and tears. She locked her arms around me, ignoring the rings from the telephone. The media was on her for another comment about my arrest. She went out on a limb, suggesting maybe the cocaine wasn't mine. Papa fiddled in the kitchen, eyeing some half-eaten lunch. Meanwhile, we sat on the couch, her tears spilling over and our pain consuming us. She would gladly take on my ache; her desire to protect me was as strong as ever.

"I'm here for you, always," Mom explained, wiping this round of tears away and adding to the mound of Kleenex. Her reminder never needed to be spoken. Since childhood, she had been a retreat from Marv's intensity. Now, she was a haven from my follies. But although she was well-intentioned, her efforts would only delay my descent to rock bottom.

After a night at Mom's house, it was time to talk with Marv—my mentor, hero, nemesis, and most brutal critic. And yet, this exchange surprised me the most, especially after news of my arrest made the front page of national papers. It was in bold print beside a headline about the start of the Gulf War. In retrospect, the irony isn't lost on me. As the country went to battle, I began my fight against addiction. Unfortunately, unlike conventional war, my addiction would never end. I'd have to learn to live with the ongoing conflict.

While I fully expected a tongue-lashing from the man whose standards knew no bounds, he took a different tack as we spoke on the phone.

"It's a bump in the road, Orange," he said, using a tried-and-true nickname as he worked to convince himself as much as me.

"What about the draft?" I asked incredulously, hoping he could pull a rabbit out of a hat. I busied my mitts with a football, but it couldn't soothe my anxiety. "Coach Smith called and told me he'd take me back."

"No need to go that way. Someone will take a chance on you if you prepare. Are you ready to put in the work?" he asked with the sobriety of a man who'd never touched a drink, smoked a joint, or done a line.

"Yes." I spoke cautiously, sensing that my athletic future was no longer a shared burden between us.

His crisp parting words were an about-face after years of intense involvement. Marv insisted, "It's your deal now, so go make the most of it. Call Benny Podda. He's your guy."

"Benny Podda?" I questioned, surprised to hear this name emerge from the archives.

"Yes, Benny." Then, just as the conversation began, it ended.

How the hell would I unearth Benny Podda? Word on the street was that he didn't want to be found. He'd taken up residence in a cabin or cave somewhere deep within Silverado Canyon. Living a monk-like existence, this enigma was not easy to reach. I'd ask around and then hunt my way through the canyons, looking for Benny along with my lost compass. But first, I needed to prepare to pay my freight in sweat. Benny was no joke. It was full-on when I entered his presence, as in ground to orbit in under ten.

Benny's a difficult cat to explain—eccentrically gifted in many regards with unorthodox methods across all aspects of life. Rumors suggested that he robbed a pharmacy using a bow and arrow and wore werewolf masks during bodybuilding competitions. He also gushed blood out of his nose at will. All tall tales, I suspect. As for the suggestion that he could hang more than two hundred pounds from his nuts, well, I never dared to ask about that one.

From firsthand experience, I knew this guy was as colorful as a box of Crayola crayons. He was a next-level medicine man, trainer, and spiritual guru. I first met Benny toward the end of high school at Marv's gym within the Anaheim Hilton. I'd finished spring practice, limping in on crutches with a badly sprained ankle. Marv's usual go-to guy, Leroy—part pharmacist, part bookie—suggested Benny for help with my condition. So it shouldn't have surprised me that Benny was in the gym, awaiting my arrival.

Full of hope, I hobbled up to this mini Mack truck. If his physique indicated his talents, I was in good hands. The guy was the perfect block of muscle, diced without an ounce of fat, with boundless energy and passion oozing from his pores. He greeted me with a firm handshake, which felt akin to handling a meat hook. Then he asked me to sit on the bench. The most bizarre thing about the experience was that Benny never touched my ankle. He created powerful heat, rubbing his palms together and hovering over the grape Popsicle–colored injury with the movement of a spaceship. It must have been an alien intervention because I could feel the heat radiating into my ankle, as if from a makeshift microwave inches from my skin. I shrugged my shoulders, still unconvinced, until I stood. I rose and gingerly applied some weight to the foot. I could walk—hell, even jog—without pain. Benny's skills defied logic, winning Marv and me over for life as I strode out of the gym, tossing the crutches.

Given this history and Marv's recommendation, I began the search for my redeemer. I headed into the canyons, conscious of the energy change from the salty smells of the ocean to the earthy aromas of the woods. I breathed deep, drawing in the scents of moist moss and peat. Leroy had given me rough directions on the back of a napkin, but it looked more like a treasure map. I followed the fire roads with periodic off-roading until I spied a truck on a distant hillside. Benny, perhaps a seer too, barreled toward me through the woods in a tan Ram truck.

"Looking for me?" he belted out from his ride as he came within earshot.

"Did you get my message?"

"Of course, good old Leroy sent a runner in between filling prescriptions and taking bets." He grinned. Leroy was as peculiar and undefinable as Benny. No wonder they were friends.

"Yup, I'm guessing you didn't hear it in the news, but I've got to get in gear for the NFL draft. Since I'm too young to enter the combine, I gotta hold my own."

Benny nodded, unfazed. He didn't share my addiction to football.

"What would it take for you to spend a few months getting me ready?" I fished.

"Nothing, just your commitment . . . and I mean unwavering dedication."

I expected nothing less, confirming with a nod.

"Good then, let's start today," he declared without blinking.

It was precisely what I'd hoped to hear. It was a good thing I had packed my bag for the duration because I would need it.

Benny dictated a few orders to prime the pump, including human growth hormone (HGH), until the draft. It would help me derive the maximum benefit from the grueling months ahead. Jabbing a needle into my ass every day was a small price to pay to achieve my goals. That shit was magic, but it was the only period of my life when I used the juice. I didn't want to bulk up too much.

Under Benny's supervision and intense preparation in his tree-ensconced home, I reached the pinnacle of my mental and physical shape. I topped out at 233 pounds and a mere 8 percent body fat. Nature was our vast dojo as I squatted logs, lifted heavy rocks, pressed into trees, and navigated trails parkour-style. I also lived on isometric holds and many slow movements based on tai chi methodologies. Wise in various practices, Benny closed each session with breathwork and mental training. By the end of our time, he deemed me a freak—though not in the conventional sense. In his unorthodox world, it was the ultimate compliment. Like Marv, Benny wouldn't follow societal norms with his praise. Instead, I had to read between the lines.

The plan of wowing teams at my mini combine took shape. As I made gains through the training protocol, my agents recruited two offensive coordinators: Mike Holmgren of the 49ers and June Jones of the Falcons—the masterminds behind my showcase. They also secured some star power in Stacey Bailey, an Atlanta Falcons veteran wideout. We spent a full day on Los Angeles Valley College's Astroturf throwing routes. By the appointed hour, it was a well-scripted show without a single ball drop.

My agents invited twenty teams to the showcase. Every one of them came to witness what I could do. I loved to perform and had a well-honed knack for making it count when it mattered most. I recall the 49ers head coach, George Seifert, eyeing my movements with interest. He asked me to try all sorts of additional tests. The more he threw at me, the better I did.

Halfway through my time with Coach Seifert, a familiar face strolled into the stadium, taking a seat between Mom and Marv:

Raiders owner Al Davis, whose cologne made an entrance well before he did. Their exchange was heartfelt—a genuine hug with Mom and a firm, respectful handshake with Marv. I breathed a sigh of relief. From Marv's experience with the Raiders, I knew Al only exerted himself for things he cared about. It looked like I might be one of them. As long as I continued to perform and impress, which was second nature by this point, I believed it was a done deal. So I dropped my shoulder back and started firing off bombs, Al's favorite. He loved the vertical game. At the end of the day, I knelt on the forty-yard line and threw the ball as far as possible. I saw a few coaches gesture out of the corner of my eye, impressed as the ball sailed through the goalposts—the perfect cherry on top of a stellar day.

While the guys in attendance took note, the national media speculated I might be taken in the twelfth round despite the arrest. A few weeks later, their conjectures evolved. They suggested possibly the sixth round, and then, a week later, the third. Finally, a few outlets got it right: they believed I had first-round selection potential.

I declined offers to fly to New York for the draft and instead checked into a Loews Santa Monica Beach Hotel suite. I wanted to hang with friends and crash out until the main event. I gave my agent, Mike Barnett—Wayne Gretzky's guy who partnered with Tom Condon—specific instructions to roust me before the Raiders were on the clock. As I celebrated into the wee hours of the morning with close friends, I wasn't feeling stressed. I'd done everything I could and more since the arrest. So I trusted the universe to bring it home. Meanwhile, I temporarily satiated my growing addiction with a half-dozen beers and Jack shooters.

The next day started like the opening scene from *The Hangover*.

There wasn't a tiger in the bathroom or a baby in the closet, but I was far from sober and hadn't had a wink of sleep. I spotted dozens of beers, several Jack Daniel's bottles, plenty of substances on the glass coffee tables, and some random clothes in the trash. Then I heard a loud rap on the door and stumbled toward the stereo. *A resort rent-a-cop?* Just in case, I silenced the music and hushed the few remaining diehards. Slowly opening the door and squinting in the stark light of the hallway, I encountered my agent. At least three coffees into his morning, Mike was jumpy and ready for action. He must have showered with a squeegee, he was so fresh-faced and polished.

"It's 5 AM, but it's about to start back east. The Raiders will be on the clock in another hour or so," Mike stated. Word on the street was that I'd be their first selection. But if they passed for whatever reason, favorable rumors had emerged from inside the New York Jets franchise.

"Oh, great. Thanks," I said, less energetically.

"You bet, now let's get you some rest." He pointed to my motley assortment of friends on the couch. They were the human Whitman's Sampler: budding artists, musicians, dancers, and athletes.

"Yeah, I could use some rest. Call me when it's time," I requested as my crew took the cue to head out.

Once everyone left, I shut the door and signed off for a short nap. Partway through a dream, the phone rang louder than a fire alarm. Guessing it was my agent, I rose and grabbed it on the fourth ring.

"Hey, Mike."

"Todd, it's Coach Shell," a deep, smooth radio voice responded. It was the Raiders' head coach. My family had known him for decades as one of Marv's early recruits for the Raiders. My heart skipped a beat.

"Hey, Coach." I cleared my throat of any party remnants. "Sorry about that."

"No sweat. I wanted to call you personally to let you know that we unanimously decided to select you as our first pick."

"Holy shit, right on, Coach. Thank you. This was the news I hoped for, and I can't wait to get after it." I left out the part about getting started after sobering up from last night's bender.

"Great. Our people will contact you with today's schedule. They're sending a car. Be ready within the hour. It's going to be a long day."

"Yes, Coach." I was jacked.

After we hung up, I ran onto the balcony and unleashed a primal scream, my body covered with goose bumps. Over a decade of grueling work had landed me at the pinnacle. The climax was short-lived, though. After a few minutes, I stepped back inside to look around the trashed hotel suite. It was time to sober up with the type of reality check only discovered in an ice-cold shower followed by a twenty-ounce dark coffee and as much electrolyte water as I could stomach. I couldn't arrive drunk on day one of a new job.

My first day as a Raider was one of the longest of my life. It began with two hours of interviews. Then the staff granted me a short time-out to peruse the facility. When I entered the still of the locker room, I locked eyes with Bo Jackson, one of the greatest athletes in the modern era. He stood, stronger than a bison but as compact as a pit bull. I couldn't believe my luck and must've been grinning from ear to ear. He was there to clean out his locker after an abbreviated but amazing run with the franchise. Much to everyone's disappointment, his time had been cut short by a career-ending injury.

In true Bo fashion, it was a brief but heartfelt exchange as the pressure of his beefy hand fell on my shoulder heavier than a slab of tri-tip. It represented the passing of weighty expectations from one star to another. He released his grip with a lightness. Wishing me luck, he flashed his soulful smile before taking one last look around. Then he literally and figuratively vanished from the public eye.

After Bo took off, I approached my locker with Christmas-like anticipation. I made out "Marinovich" above the locker: a tangible sign that instantly made the whole experience real. The spot was mine. I'd earned it. I'd be playing in the NFL—not hoping or watching—while throwing the ball to some of the game's greats, including Tim Brown and Willie Gault. I'd also hand off to several of the best running backs in the business: Marcus Allen, Roger Craig, and Eric Dickerson. This was all I wanted from football: to play among the best.

Handing off to Marcus Allen.

Eyeing the jersey a bit closer, I stutter-stepped, and my eyes narrowed: number sixteen. *Come on. Really?* I didn't want to seem ungrateful—I loved Jim Plunkett—but I wasn't a number sixteen guy. It was a momentary disappointment, though. I immediately zeroed in on a man who could fix anything, the receiver coach and former player Fred Biletnikoff. He was a wily coyote who made a living catching balls from Ken Stabler. He was also a fixture in Raiders lore and a former teammate of Marv's on the 1965 roster.

"Look what they gave me," I shared, holding the jersey as a billboard for Fred to see from across the locker room.

Fred squinted but didn't say a thing. He strolled over with a half-finished cigarette hanging from his lips, equally unclear and unbothered as the smoke lingered in his wake.

"Don't get me wrong, Plunkett was great." I launched into an off-the-cuff explanation. But Fred wasn't listening. He handed me a fresh cigarette instead.

"Relax, kid, I got you," he interrupted, tossing me a lighter as the edges of his mouth curled like the Cheshire cat's mischievous grin.

How does he know that I smoke? I was up to at least a pack of Marlboros a day.

"I'm a Snake guy, man." I hoped he'd read between the lines. "Thanks for the cig," I added, realizing this was a guy to keep in my corner. I'd eventually have more than a cigarette to thank him for, as he would do his best to keep me focused during my brief tenure with the Raiders.

Fred paused, took another long drag, and brought me to the phone. He dropped the receiver into my palm. "Well, call Kenny, then. Make it happen."

My nerves spiked as he rattled off his digits. I waited a

hellishly long moment before entering the last number. *Fuck it, what do I have to lose but my pride?*

Moments later, Ken picked up, offering the most gracious southern gentleman greeting. He sounded light-years away from the hellion quarterback of his youth.

I paused, then introduced myself and explained my predicament. "How'd you feel about me wearing your number instead?" I probed cautiously.

"I'd be honored, Todd," he responded without hesitation.

And so began my Raiders career as number twelve. I channeled my childhood hero and another leftie quarterback, the wild and rebellious Ken "the Snake" Stabler.

Raiders rookie year, 1991.

Even with everything falling into place, it didn't take long for my insatiable love of football and drugs to barrel toward a head-on collision. With Hollywood celebrities on speed dial and more temptations than in Sodom and Gomorrah, everything was far too accessible in my hometown. Looking back, I was doomed the moment I donned that Raiders jersey. But it all felt ready-made at the time. I moved seamlessly from USC to the Raiders, even playing at the Coliseum for both teams. With the universe seemingly working in my favor, I wanted to show my appreciation, celebrating far and wide. And I certainly did, with reckless abandon.

Before training camp, one of the all-pro veterans called with clear instructions: "Bring a couple of ounces of crip to camp."

I paused, too stunned to answer this force of nature. I wondered how many of my new teammates smoked weed.

He persisted. "I know you went to USC. I'm sure you've got good connections, so come loaded."

"All right, I got you," I said, my initial shock morphing into excitement. If this call was any indication, I was in for a good time with like-minded brothers. So I arrived with plenty of pot and a surfboard on top of the Land Cruiser, ready to crank it up.

Later, at the end of training camp in August 1991, I went all out in hosting my first NFL party. It was a true barn burner. It was customary for recruits to throw a rager at the close of camp, and this one had to be legendary. Treating my assignment off the field like a nosy reporter, I probed players about infamous parties. What were the wildest stunts? The franchise had a long, colorful history of crazy antics. They were the rule-defying, anything-goes renegades who thrived outside the lines—the team was sometimes called the NFL's halfway house. It wasn't far from the truth, especially in the 1970s.

Back in the John Madden era, they partied harder than nearly any other team in the league. With Coach giving players plenty of slack off the field, rebels Ken "the Snake" Stabler, Ted "the Mad Stork" Hendricks, and the unhinged John "Tooz" Matuszak would go to town literally and figuratively. I heard it was like shaking a beer can and letting it rip after the last meeting of the night. Highlights from these escapades, namely bras, panties, and a carpet of beer cans, decorated training camp suites. But one player dared to blur the boundaries. Preferring to make an entrance, the Mad Stork galloped in on horseback at the start of one practice, dismounting like a medieval knight on the fifty-yard line. Rumor has it that Madden didn't even flinch since these pranks were so common.

With plenty of outlandish history as my guide, I designed a party for the ages. I even pulled in Mom to assist with some of the arrangements. She was always ready to take on any burden.

"I'm throwing a big party at the end of camp and need some help," I seeded during an innocuous call after my sixth two-a-day practice of week one.

"A party? Of course. What do you need?" She was all in. A former USC sorority girl and natural party planner, she scouted locations and planned the menu with a mother's passion.

Meanwhile, I covertly managed the rest of the stuff that would've dropped her jaw. And I knew who to call to support that part of the equation. Juan was my usual contact, moving high quantities of drugs. He always gave me whatever I wanted in exchange for tickets to USC football games.

"Hey man, it's Todd. I've got a boatload of Raiders to impress. Can you help me out?"

"Hell yeah. For you and the frickin' Raiders, anything. I'll set you up with whatever you want."

"I need plenty of weed and coke," I rattled off like Escobar's personal shopper.

"That's easy—anything else?" he probed.

"Any chance I could get the stuff in two days?"

I met him at the appointed hour in Costco's parking lot.

"You always come through for me," I said, thanking him as he dropped a bag in the back seat. With the 11 PM curfew a distant memory, I snuck back into camp undetected shortly after 1:30 AM. I was hoping for a catnap as my mind drifted, and the walls eventually danced me to sleep.

Meanwhile, Mom found the perfect spot for the revelry: a secluded ranch in Oxnard, California. It was out of the paparazzi's reach and close to training camp. The large spread had a massive barn, the perfect spot for off-the-wall entertainment. My inner artist went to work immediately. I envisioned something akin to a circus with hay bales as stadium bleachers for unobstructed views of center stage. An impressive DJ booth and a peppering of well-stocked bars flanked the space.

But what would keep everyone's eyes glued to the main stage? For that, I went to one of the veterans. He was more straitlaced than the others, rarely drinking, and quick to speed off from camp in a sweet ride. But he knew his guys and understood I hoped to make a lasting impression.

"I want the team to remember the night long after—to top the list of the best camp party ever," I admitted, knowing it would be difficult to wow players who had everything at their disposal.

"I'm going to give you two numbers," he responded. "Don't ask questions. Just call both to get things handled."

I nodded my appreciation and pocketed the information. The first was a contact who lined up a dozen strippers. The second one caught me off guard. It was a contact in the adult film industry who secured a half-dozen porn stars for the event.

These professionals, well versed in rousing audiences of testosterone-and-alcohol-fueled dudes, needed little instruction. I watched the crowd from the cheap seats as the party kicked into gear. The strippers took on act one, and the film stars got creative with their bodies in act two. They did things with toys that some of these farm boys had never seen or imagined.

Even I didn't anticipate what came next. The strippers and porn stars, not unlike NFL teams, were highly competitive when performing. Who could get more audience response? Which side could push it further? It turned into one hell of a dance-off with the two groups raising the stakes with a mind-blowing finale worthy of a porn Oscar.

After ninety minutes of arousal, the crowd was electric, with more androgens cresting than at a prizefight. Not wanting to leave these red-blooded guys hanging, the entertainers formed small huddles. They performed acts in unholy positions that wives and girlfriends could never know. I must protect the not-so-innocent, but it would be fair to say almost everyone came away satisfied.

Meandering outside the barn to the barbecue, I discovered plenty of linemen who prioritized the buffet over the girls. My forethought was rewarded, as I'd secured the best grill masters. With the carcasses of a fully carved cow and a pig, it was a meat fest—a paleo eater's wet dream. My guys were lions, gorging on an endless quest to maintain their bulk. It was a selfish act of giving: keeping them well fed with nonstop ribs and steaks would protect me from brutal sacks on the turf once the regular season started.

All told, the $15,000 spent on the mayhem was well worth it.

In the following days, messages blew up my phone filled with stories that lived on, like the one about the strippers who accompanied two players home for a marathon session. Or the teammate who naively tried dating one of the porn stars—that's right, love, or lust, didn't last. Then there was my teammate who got in deep shit with his wife for arriving home days after camp wrapped. I guess he went on a bender, but I'd never tell. To avoid the same fate, another famous veteran insisted, "Awesome party, but I was never there, right?" There were too many names and countless reputations to protect in the aftermath.

They say that first impressions matter, and while I'd certainly delivered a memorable experience for my teammates, the party had also rewarded my own extreme tendencies. But with camp in the rearview mirror and the season set to begin, I had to get my head straight. This was a far greater challenge than all the physical training. I packed my bags, cruised to my new townhouse in Manhattan Beach, and spent the afternoon staring at the empty walls of the bedroom. I felt as vacant as that barren space, with Jack Daniel's keeping my thoughts at bay, if only for a night. While being alone is not the same as feeling alone, I was both as I headed into the most intense period of my life.

Once the season was into its weekly rhythm, I really wanted out of my skin as I grew increasingly weary of my inescapable public identity. Media scrutiny had made me uncomfortable in high school and at USC, but it only intensified as a Raider. The long shadow of judgment followed me everywhere. I couldn't eat at restaurants or walk down streets without attention of all sorts: favorable, nasty, and everything in between. With each passing day, the public persona of Todd Marinovich felt as unfamiliar as a foreign crossword puzzle. It was an odd feeling to be a stranger in my physical form, but that's how I felt most days, especially when I was sober.

The media onslaught.

After many nuanced attempts, I rebelled at one practice by impersonating Jimi Hendrix. Why pretend to be one of the greatest artists of all time? I admired his unconventional ways and life outside the lines. And our backgrounds had a few common threads, including a quick rise to fame far too early. It would be fair to say that neither of us handled it well.

On Halloween eve—shortly after a drubbing by the Kansas City Chiefs—I threw a party with some USC friends. They were in their junior year, as I would have been if the disastrous Sun Bowl fiasco had never happened. Carefree and always up for a party, former Trojan teammates, track stars, and many budding artists filled my beach pad. Pods toggled between the yard, beer pong in the spacious living room, and relays to the bars a street north on Highland Avenue.

As the party began, I applied my final touches on an hours-long metamorphosis, painting nuanced tones of browns and blacks on everything but my back and lower belly. At the time, it honestly never crossed my mind that someone might find my blackface inappropriate, but now as I look back, I'm deeply sorry for that careless oversight. My efforts were intended to honor, not demean, one of my heroes. I finished the look with platform shoes, hip-hugger bell-bottoms, a flowered flowing shirt, an afro, and a boa around my neck. I was transformed. The crowd welcomed Jimi Hendrix to the festivities.

As the night escalated and ecstasy coursed through my veins, the cops came to break up the gathering. Hearing a hard rap at the door, most of my crew scattered faster than pigeons while I manned the foyer. These soft, beach boy cops demanded to see Todd Marinovich.

"That's me," I insisted.

"Yeah right, kid. Seriously, get us Todd Marinovich," they pushed, impatiently shifting their weight from foot to foot.

I shrugged, backed away to find my wallet, and returned with my California ID in hand. Then I took my forefinger and dragged it across my forehead, exposing pale, freckled skin under my paint job. "It's me," I reiterated.

"No way," the junior cop in the back blurted out. The older bluebird in front turned to shoot him a look of death.

"It's just a little gathering of friends." I was trying to downplay the party as a hottie track star breezed by in a jet-black thong catsuit. It was perfect timing, just enough to take the edge off these cops.

"Sure, Todd," he said, still eyeing my friend. "Especially after that loss—ouch."

Great. Everyone in my path was an armchair quarterback. But I lucked out with only a citation for disturbing the peace, the most benign thing on my growing record. Not long after, the Manhattan Beach neighborhood would band together to sign a petition: my out-of-control gatherings were too much for the 'hood to handle.

By the morning, my body was dancing with a blissful cocktail of ecstasy and booze. Despite my haze, the alarm clock shook me from the Jacuzzi at 7:40 AM, and I reluctantly pulled my naked body to attention. Everything in me resisted, but my mind played the good cop for once. I couldn't blow off practice, not in the pros. There were no acceptable excuses for missing. I'd crawl or show up in an ambulance if necessary.

I stepped out of the Jacuzzi tub and immediately noticed that I was every shade of brown, black, and coffee. Paint dripped from my skin. I was literally melting—or was my mind playing tricks? I looked back at the tub, which now resembled a vat of Hershey's syrup with a floating Barbie. *A hallucination?* Ecstasy wouldn't cause me to trip. I was about to plunge my head into the gooey chocolate mess when my Barbie stated decisively, "You're going to practice as Jimi fucking Hendrix." She shimmied in giddy anticipation. I was never one to disappoint.

Raiders practice would begin in twenty short minutes. Living close to the El Segundo facility, I'd have to show up flying higher than air. Nothing at my disposal could sober me up in time. So I embraced my altered reality, touched up my paint job, put my outfit on, and let my body's autopilot deliver me—a package with a pulse. At precisely 7:59 AM, Jimi Hendrix entered the facility as if he owned the place. Beat that, Mad Stork.

As I approached the line, one of my teammates blurted out,

"Holy shit—look at the blue-eyed brother." I smiled and waved like a celebrity on tour. I was still too high to question if they noticed my condition. Instead, I grabbed the first ball I saw and let it rip: a beautifully clean spiral. I could do practically anything high, even football. Then I turned to watch Coach Shell close his eyes and slowly shake his head. Like John Madden decades ago, he took it in stride. It was just another chapter in Raiders lore.

After a few throws, Fred sauntered by, inching close to whisper, "The Stork's got nothing on you, buddy." He'd know, having seen it all.

I fell in with the other quarterbacks—strong-armed Jay Schroeder and the supremely athletic Vince Evans—to work on our agility as we navigated a minefield of dummies. I treated it like a late-night obstacle course at the clubs—no problem. Then we moved on to practicing our drop-backs and throwing routes as I spent more time watching figures form in the clouds. Remarkably, no one questioned my sobriety, not a single coach or player. I showed up on time, which counted for something.

After practice wrapped, I cruised south on the 405 Freeway to camp out at a spot with guaranteed anonymity: the surf point at the San Onofre nuclear power plant in North San Diego County. It sounds like a risky place to get in the water until you see the waves at this gem. The point break, marked by two crazy-looking massive silos affectionately called "the Boobs," is an easy-to-overlook desert wasteland. Yet the rough terrain drops from a steep hillside, meeting a surprisingly steady Waikiki-style wave. With an early-fall swell in effect, I had to convene with Mother Blue.

At first light, I shed my board shorts and paddled out naked from trail four with determined remoteness. I literally stripped myself of Todd Marinovich. I needed to be one with the creator. With the dark receding and the soft light of day easing off the horizon, I was in awe; the majesty of the universe was on full display as pastel paint dripped from the sky into liquid blackness. But as peaceful as it was, my thoughts were always my tormentors, and substances were the only assassins.

Sitting Zen-like on my longboard, I watched the waves to determine which were friend or foe. If only I could have deciphered my thoughts with the same precision. My mind was an echo chamber: *Must I do what I am good at? Or can I un-become myself and be free?* With no clarity, I enjoyed the brief respite. But I'd suffer until I could answer these questions with a clear mind and self-love.

Chapter Three

Bred to Be?

"Marv." Who calls their dad by their first name without being a little fucked up? Most of the time, he scared the shit out of people. With his stare that could dig holes and his predatory posture, it was best to fall in line or get the hell out of the way. He operated with one goal in mind: athletic success. And with that mission, he drove a literal and figurative bulldozer through our house to achieve it.

I was ten years old when I found myself surrounded by men larger than our refrigerator. I'd run out of the kitchen to avoid getting trapped into girl talk with Mom and my older sister, Traci. They spoke in tongues. My sister was about to cry, all puffy-eyed and sorrowful. All I had to catch was "bad boyfriend," and they lost me faster than a plate of organ meat. I busted open the door to the garage to check on Dad. He held court with four Rams players, reviewing the day's training sequence. As their huddle broke, I caught one of the guys, with skin blacker than night, joking with Dad.

"You're the only cracker I know named Marvin." He laughed and shook his head in disbelief.

"Yeah, I hear that all the time." Dad offered a shit-eating grin. He pointed to the bench, a visual cue that it was time to get busy.

"Okay, Marv, I got you. Time to sweat." The literal people mover, an offensive lineman known for his brick wall of a torso, took his position on the bench.

With everyone else calling him Marv, I decided to try it out too. Why not? After a moment of hesitation, I went for it: "Hey, Marv," I hollered from the other end of the garage, intentionally near the driveway in case I needed to make a quick getaway.

Dad paused. It was long, maybe two seconds. You could've heard a pin drop as chatter abruptly stopped.

I wondered if I still had time to grab my Huffy bike before hightailing it out of there. I pivoted and froze. Dad's head snapped. He and the other guys examined me intensely before laughing louder than cracking glass.

My heart raced. I was a rat cornered in a cage as my eyes darted from Marv to my bike.

"Okay, Red Rocket, you can call me Marv too," he replied with more accumulated affection than I'd received in weeks, maybe months.

I smiled. "Okay, Marv," I said, testing it out again as my lips met awkwardly and the sound slipped into the air. For the next thirty years he was Marv, never again Dad. He was a paladin and antihero, all wrapped into one remarkable force of nature.

Marv's high bar for everyone in his life began with the man in the mirror. He played football at USC as captain of the 1962 national championship team. Then he was drafted by both the NFL and AFL when they were separate leagues. Choosing between the Rams and the Raiders was an easy decision. Marv detected another near genius in Al Davis and established a relationship lasting decades. After leaving the NFL, he returned to the Raiders as the league's first sports and conditioning coach. When Al's son and the Raiders' current owner Mark Davis said, "Todd was born a Raider," he wasn't kidding. Having spent my formative years traipsing around their facility, I had the team in my blood and nature.

Early signs of my future, 1971.

Marv possessed superhero strength; in his twenties, he squatted over a thousand pounds multiple times and performed a bevy of other weight-lifting feats. Yet he felt misled by conventional wisdom. Bench-pressing heavier weight didn't help him on the field; it had the opposite effect. After three years, overtraining ended his NFL career prematurely. This turned his inner campfire into a conflagration. He was compelled to answer two age-old questions in sports: How do you get the most out of an athlete? And could a nonathlete become one with the proper training?

As Marv perfected the methods of Marinovich Training Systems, a name not coined until much later, I benefited but sometimes paid the price. His garage laboratory became my dojo at age seven—yes, you got that right: I was in second grade. Timmy, my imaginary friend, was spared, though. He got to stay in my room and play with G.I. Joe while I popped my cherry doing Russian getups.

The garage was all grit with nothing on the walls but decades-old white paint inching toward a Coventry Gray. There was no fancy equipment in the space—that candy-ass shit turned Marv into a mad hornet. Machines were forbidden in the sanctum because no motion in life was that uniform. Instead, the garage was full of hidden, multifunctional gems. I spent hours on balance boards, juggling and twisting into awkward positions, mimicking origami folds with my body while reciting my multiplication tables. Why work the body and not the mind too? It was a game, at least for the first few years. The multipronged challenges were original, and Marv's brilliant mind was hard to dismiss. Sure, he was a strength coach by trade, but he was also a creative genius and a self-taught scientist.

Beyond the balance boards, I used discarded lumberyard planks and benches for specialized shoeless footwork. Marv's foot fetish was something to behold. The first twenty minutes of every session focused exclusively on the feet. After that work was behind me, I occasionally used free weights, but rarely the heavy stuff and never in linear motions. Twists, turns, arcs, angles: while it was all based on science, it often felt more like art.

Marv also had a universal assessment system, believing there were three levels of athlete: JV, Varsity, and All–Solar System, which few earned. He actually applied this "good, better, best" mentality to nearly everything in his life, from apples to gyms and on-field performances. He was often quick to inform me when my practice or game was JV. I recall one late-night football practice when my effort was entirely too JV for his liking, so he forced me to run the eight miles home, lit by the beams of his headlights. Brutal? Maybe, but I was in such great cardiovascular shape that I could've easily run twice that distance. I absorbed his verbal jabs like a champ. I buried them so deep that the layers of explosives didn't detonate until they were lit and fueled by addiction decades later.

To be fair, though, Marv was genuinely impartial. While he rarely called my performances All–Solar System, when he did, I knew he meant it. These included my final win over UCLA during my sophomore year at USC, the 1990 Rose Bowl, and the win over Washington State in 1989, which also caught President Reagan's attention. While a call from the leader of the free world was great, I'd take Marv's All–Solar System compliment over that any day. I rode on one of the best natural highs for days after earning Marv's greatest praise.

After I left football and took a break from training in the mid-1990s, Marv opened several gyms and met a young Oregonian hopeful who became his ultimate prized pupil. Troy Polamalu, the NFL Hall of Fame strong safety, demonstrated unmatched athleticism under Marv's watchful eye. After dominating at USC, Troy was the first safety picked in the 2003 draft. Then he won two Super Bowl rings and earned five consecutive trips to the Pro Bowl. As Marv would say, Troy was undeniably All–Solar System.

Troy later referred to Marv as "the king" and "a savant" for his exceptional strength and conditioning coaching talents. But he also expressed the importance of staying within Marv's good graces. Marv required textbook obedience and steel-like mental strength. Troy watched plenty of guys fall to the wayside after only a session or two. They dared to complain instead of "loading the wagon," as Marv would say. And forget about it if they carried a Gatorade into the temple.

Along with rigorous training, Marv believed that a clean and regimented diet was essential to achieving superior outcomes. He often rifled through his pupils' lunch bags. Like a Rottweiler rooting out treats, he would sniff out any contraband, rattling on about being unable to out-train a bad diet.

Marv's book, *ProBodX*, short for Proper Body Exercise, detailed his well-honed approach to building and toning muscle while increasing strength, flexibility, and balance. The program, a culmination of decades of experimentation on me and others, combined unstable surfaces with multiplane activity and strength loading. This recipe both elongated and strengthened the body. It also led to a more activated nervous system. It increased quickness, power, and plasticity. Marv believed that to be a top athlete, one had to perform in all areas and toggle with fluidity—one needed the ability to "relax and fire." His philosophy even captured the attention of Alex Guerrero, Tom Brady's body coach, who reached out to learn the Marinovich system.

Marv's greatest epiphany was the discovery that the nervous system held the key to the castle, firing everything of matter. This revelation ushered in the future of sports training. The 1 percent in the know got it. But there were still plenty of leaders and programs clinging to the past. It tormented Marv to no end. He'd cringe hearing that top universities had built million-dollar weight rooms to train athletes as if they were bodybuilders and powerlifters. Meanwhile, he discarded 90 percent of his heavy weights.

Despite the anguish of seeing top athletes injured through ignorance, Marv could rest knowing that he had answers to both of his initial questions: proper body exercise could get the most out of a competitor, and even a nonathlete could become Varsity with the right training. This shattered the prevailing belief system that a person was born an athlete.

No one proved the latter point more profoundly than Dylan, a short, uncoordinated, and pudgy kid who began training with Marv in seventh grade. Cast off by coaches as more appropriate for nonathletic extracurriculars, Marv dug in deep with Dylan. After six disciplined years of training, he was the demonstration guy. He performed the system for trainers, the media, and new pupils. He was truly Varsity, transforming into a formidable stud—an All–Orange County linebacker for Mater Dei High School. If there were any doubters of Marv's methods, Dylan proved them all wrong.

Meanwhile, the media never saw the hundreds of young women Marv quietly trained over the decades. He appreciated that they didn't have the big egos of their male counterparts.

They would train just as hard, if not harder, than the boys. Untold numbers of remarkable female athletes earned sports scholarships in part because of Marv. There was no fanfare or public accolade, but his generous gift of time had profound effects on these young lives.

Despite Marv's intensity and obsession with performance, I never had a single house chore and was rarely disciplined. And instead of using the belt, Marv would hand me boxing gloves to go at it in the backyard, beginning at twelve years old. Occasionally, he recruited older kids from the neighborhood to fight me. But most of the time it was just Marv and me working it out in the makeshift ring.

The dread would mount each time he instructed me to get the boxing gloves. I'd feel like I was walking in deep sand. I would slowly make my way to the door, wondering if any excuse would fly. It never did. And despite knowing how the match would unfold, I still dreaded it. It opened the same way without fail: I would protect myself as Marv antagonized me with soft body punches. Entrenched in a defensive mindset, I wouldn't fight back at this point. But after a while, the barrage would work me into a fury of purple rage. Eventually, I'd lash out. Seeing me flushing, frothing at the mouth, and firing away would drive Marv to hysterical laughter. Ten minutes in, I'd be too exhausted to continue. Whatever tension existed before the match would vaporize. Like animals, we worked out our issues without words.

But it didn't go quite the same way with other kids. One

matchup and highway beatdown affair is etched into my memory like cave art. It was a rare lazy Saturday afternoon. Marv strolled into the garage with Mike, an upperclassman built as solid as an Abrams tank. Marv tossed me the gloves and handed Mike his pair with a gladiator-style nod. Forget pleasantries; it was time to get busy. *Oh shit.*

I poked and jabbed, but my bony little arms were like rubber bands. I was grazing the target, barely moving the wall of gristle. Meanwhile, Mike circled me, seventh-grade veal. Trying to tune out Marv, who perpetually coached me ringside, I missed any warning. Mike made contact with a solid smack, pasting me to the floor. With just one punch, the match ended. More than anything, I was relieved that the baby cockfight was over. Mike took the opportunity to exit stage left, leaving me to face Marv's frustration. But he surprised me for once without his usual verdict of a JV performance.

"Taco time?" he asked, heading to the Volkswagen.

I jumped at the opportunity for a treat—a radical deviation from the far-too-common pan-seared chicken breast, brown rice, and steamed vegetables served at our kitchen table. But as we pulled out of our neighborhood and onto a busy thoroughfare in Newport Beach, he was itching to hit something more his size. I prayed for a quick ride.

I wasn't so lucky this time. A cherry-red Camaro flipped him off while flying by in the slow lane. Marv accelerated and slid in behind the bravado-filled dick, inching dangerously close. The Camaro tapped the brakes, the universal signal to fuck off. Swerving into the left lane, Marv would get even. In every facet of life, he was all gas and no brake. So, instead of heeding the Camaro's warning, he sped up, spewing all sorts of expletives.

Spittle rained down on me as I melted into the leather and inched my body closer to the floor mats.

Marv was in luck that day; the guy was eager for a tussle too. He bolted out of his car, and Marv met him halfway in a raging firestorm. His adversary was at least ten years his junior with far too much insecurity to take on a mad dog. Marv clocked him twice in the stomach, spun around, and returned to the car as if he had just feasted. Meanwhile, the guy was bent over, gasping for air. At my impressionable age, I could see that fighting, the real stuff, unlike what we did in the garage and backyard, made Marv come alive. That's where we were fundamentally different: I was a competitor but, at my core, a lover, not a fighter. *Would this man, who cared for me fiercely, ever understand that?*

But even if he never grasped my aversion, Marv's days as a brawler were numbered. He careened headlong into a come-to-Jesus moment about a year later in Huntington Beach. After this doozy, his public smackdowns stopped cold turkey, much to the relief of everyone in the family.

I was in middle school and playing basketball whenever and wherever I could. A regular at the Edison Community Center's half-courts in Huntington Beach, California, I played pickup ball against older kids to improve my game. On one particularly warm night, things got hot quickly. My oversized teen opponent came at me hard with egregious body checks and elbows flying. It felt like I was in a boxing ring rather than on a court. Marv finally had enough of all the flagrant fouls coming my way.

"Are you going to let that kid get away with this?" Marv hollered from half-court.

"Oh fuck," I muttered under my breath. I knew what came next. I reluctantly dropped the ball midplay, pivoted, and squared off to my opponent with my peashooters raised into position. It was best to get this over with as quickly as possible. The odds weren't in my favor. The older kid flicked the switch and released his inner monster.

I sensed a crowd forming as the space took on new energy. Meanwhile, Marv shape-shifted into the master of ceremonies. He directed the crowd to "back the fuck up" while the circle around us tightened. His eyes shot daggers, and his signature A-framed eyebrows arched like Jack Nicholson's in *The Shining*. I didn't have to look; his crazy fight face was a permanent stain in my mind.

As I assumed my signature protective position, Marv unleashed his pent-up fury on an onlooker. Hearing the commotion, I turned just in time to watch a guy raising his racket for a cheap shot at Marv. He didn't hesitate, reacting with animal instincts. Marv punched the guy straight in the mouth with a Foreman-style bomb before the racket could make it within two feet of his head. He clocked the guy so hard that it rattled the teeth from his mouth—his choppers rained down on the court like used ammunition.

After the shock passed, the crowd came raging at Marv with a vengeance.

"Fucking run, Red, meet at the car," he yelled as he turned to sprint, beelining it for the VW and leaving me in his wake, though not far behind. He had the engine going as I skidded into the passenger side faster than a *Dukes of Hazzard* renegade. Marv peeled out of the lot as the first of the crowd caught our dust and exhaust along with our license plate number. We barely escaped, but it was downhill from there.

I affixed my poker-chip-sized eyes to the wheel to follow the blood trickling down Marv's hands from open teeth marks peppering his knuckles. He turned, mildly out of breath, and flashed a twisted grin. Meanwhile, my jaw practically hit the floor mat. I couldn't digest the rapid unwinding of an innocent pickup game. This was no after-school special, that was for sure. *Mom's in for a surprise when we get home*, I thought, shuddering.

By the time we reached the front door, cop cars were approaching in code two mode, lighting up our cul-de-sac and attracting plenty of looky-loos. A bit more than a surprise, the mortifying visit left Mom in knots.

"What were you thinking?" she asked, exasperated. She pointed her finger at me as she spoke directly to Marv. Her issue was twofold: the legal disaster that would befall the family and her husband's less-than-model behavior.

Marv ignored her, not answering and stomping off to shower, muttering something indecipherable. Meanwhile, I was still saucer-eyed. Mom grabbed her purse and keys.

"Wanna come with me to Gramma and Papa's for the night?" she asked, hoping I'd make the right decision. I paused, caught in an unfair position. I'd disappoint one parent that night. But it wasn't a tough call, given my options to stay home with a pissed-off Rottweiler or enjoy a night of buttered popcorn and movies with Mom, Gramma, and Papa. I grabbed my schoolbag and bolted to her car. Off we went for a temporary respite with no peace accord in sight.

Not surprisingly, there were severe consequences for Marv's

fight. Beyond a mark on his record, he was heftily sued by the victim. This sent our family further into a financial hole. Money was always tight, but courting disaster with this recklessness made our ascent out of the rabbit hole nearly impossible.

In those early years, I couldn't fully appreciate the family strain caused by Marv's bizarre actions. While he rested comfortably in the extremes, both ends of the spectrum whipsawed our family for years. For example, he'd drop everything, putting untold miles on his old VW to shuttle kids between counties for games. And yet, he would forgo work to make it happen, even when our family's accounts were in the red. Depending on your perspective, it was an act of generosity or negligence. Over time, I realized both were true. This brings me to the plethora of contradictions within the man who shaped me: Marv was a saint and a sinner. A lover and a fighter. The man I admired most in the world and someone whose tongue felt like a switchblade to my heart. Marv never said he loved me, but I knew it. Was that enough?

And yet sometimes, paradoxically, I wished he loved me less.

My mom, Trudi (née Fertig), was the polar opposite of Marv. She was an effusive bundle of love. She freely gave and expressed with her whole heart. The quintessential Southern California girl, perpetually glowing with sparkling brown eyes and matching brown locks, she was an athlete in her own right. A specialist in the butterfly, she took home more than her fair share of country-club swimming medals throughout her teen years. Meanwhile, her older brother, Craig, was USC's star quarterback and a teammate of her future husband.

Marv didn't date sorority girls, and Trudi had no interest in linemen. But when Marv decided to marry Trudi, he bent her to his will to make it happen. So, by her sophomore year, she'd dropped out of USC. Instead of school, she focused on building a promising life with a man who would ultimately bring her both intense joy and anguish.

Mom was my greatest protector during the early years. While she rarely defied Marv, she went full tilt when she did. In some ways, she was more resilient than anyone else in the house. And she knew when to call for backup. One time, Mom got some reinforcements from the medical community. I was in junior high, back when Marv was working for the Rams, and laid up on the couch with flu-like symptoms. I was in such rough shape that Marv took me to work for an evaluation by a team doctor. I don't recall the tests, but I do remember Centinela Hospital, where I spent the night as a human pincushion.

Marv didn't seem too worried, but when Mom found out I was in the hospital, she hightailed it up the 405 Freeway to keep watch. Before she arrived, the staff moved me from the pediatric ward. Now surrounded by adult patients, I wondered what all the fuss was about.

The doctor asked Mom to bring my daily supplements so he could run some tests. I could hear them conferring right outside my door.

"How often does he take these?" the doctor asked with concern. I could hear the pill bottles shake, louder than baby rattles.

"Just once a day," Mom explained plainly, seemingly unconcerned since the entire family took something.

"Supplements?" he questioned.

"Yes." Things went quiet for a few seconds. Then I saw Mom's head peek in and disappear, followed by the hiss of hushed tones trailing off as she and the doctor walked down the hall to finish their conversation.

Well, it turns out that these Eastern bloc crazy-shit pills were the source of my troubles. They were worrisome enough that the doctors ran brain scans, checking for tumors. No one ever fully explained what was in them, but from then on, there were no more Russian-labeled pill bottles in the daily lineup.

Mom wasn't just concerned with my physical well-being; she kept a close watch on my emotional state too. One Friday afternoon after football season ended, she picked me up from school. She took one look at my withdrawn face and pulled the parachute. "How about going to the Hotel del Coronado for the weekend, just you and me, kiddo?" she half asked, half told me.

"It'll be fun," Mom continued with her razzle-dazzle Delta Gamma voice that complemented her sparkling eyes. I wondered if I'd ever find someone as beautiful as her.

Everything in me felt light in an instant. "Until Monday?" I asked, wanting to stay there as long as possible. It was our favorite getaway spot.

"Yup, I'll drop you at school on the drive home Monday morning," she confirmed.

I paused for a long while, watching the brown hues off the highway fuse into a kaleidoscope of dead leaves. "Is Marv coming too?" I fished.

"Nope." She was firm on that point. "I'll just leave him a note."

Mom moved with urgency as we packed our bags. Then she penned something as short as a grocery list to Marv. We were back on the highway in under thirty minutes. We sang along to the radio, our windows down as we passed over the San Diego–Coronado Bay Bridge, without a care in the world or a cloud in the sky.

"No rules this weekend," she stated as our car tires kissed the island.

I stared at her, the person I cared for most in the world. I couldn't imagine ever loving anyone more. "No rules," I parroted back. It sounded, looked, and tasted like freedom as we stopped for celebratory ice cream cones. The heavenly real stuff, in fresh waffle cones, not some healthy version made with unpasteurized milk and honey.

It was two days of nonstop beach, eating anything on the menu and sleeping in as long as I wanted. The time was priceless—as was the look on Marv's face on Monday night. Was he pissed? His eyebrows practically touched his hairline, and his mouth twitched in some form of Morse code. SOS for damn sure. We were on notice. And Marv had a brutal technique for sharing his dissatisfaction. He iced Mom out, refusing to speak to her. Instead, he relayed messages through me or Traci at the dinner table.

"Tell your mother to get some more milk," he seethed, glaring at me while sitting one chair away from Mom.

My eyes flitted from Marv to Mom. She didn't even flinch. She cut her string beans in silence. It seemed that she might relish the reprieve from direct engagement with Marv for as long as possible. But Marv kept on, devoid of an off switch. "Tell Chubby to get more milk, damn it."

Mom's cheeks turned red, but she kept cutting. She looked at Traci and asked about her homework. But no matter how hard she tried to disguise it, this had to hurt: Marv belittling her in plain view. It was a psychological punishment I logged as something to avoid.

I also took on the responsibility of preventing these episodes as often as possible, a tall order with a steamroller like Marv in the house. I soon discovered that performing was the best way to keep the peace. That alone kept him happy and the family intact. It was a burden I carried far too long, resulting in some serious baggage on my back and confusion lodged in my heart for decades.

Chapter Four

A Bloody Spiral

My signature throw was conceived on September 6, 1978. I had no idea that I was actually duck hunting.

It was a flawless early-fall day—cool on the ends and warm in the middle. I woke at 6:45 AM, wound into a ball of anticipation. I eyed the crisp, all-white uniform. I was a proud member of the Newport Beach Cheyennes. At nine years old, I would play in my first tackle football scrimmage. There wouldn't be any more flag stroking and four-leaf clover searching. Little did I know, however, that my debut in the big time would be nothing short of a bloodbath.

Marv met me at my bedroom door in his gray sweats, examining his Casio watch. "Time to get out of first gear," he declared with more energy than my fourth-grade class at recess.

I knew the drill. It was the Spartan warrior credo: the one who sweats more in training bleeds less in war—at least, that was the theory. We'd complete some footwork and light cardio before 7:30 AM. But first, I had to stomach the dreaded shamrock shake. It was named after its shocking green hue that put fresh clovers to shame. Chock-full of spirulina, it tasted like—no, it *was*—swamp water. As sure as sunrise, an algae-like film and a healthy amount of grainy bee pollen lingered on my tongue. After downing my doses with ritualistic discipline, my green mustache and I marched toward Marv. It was time to get busy in the dojo.

I followed his instructions to the letter, nearing autopilot it was so familiar. I was barefoot on the balance board, wiggling my body like a snake climbing a hill. Side to side I went, altering my angle and dropping back. It tested my ability to bring the board into balance—an experience of adversity for the body that mirrored life. I had to adjust, pivot, and rediscover my center. After ten minutes of board time, we ran some suicides on the grass. Then we polished it off with a half-mile jog. It was nothing rigorous, just enough to get my body humming.

I could smell my morning reward as we crossed the pavement into the garage at 7:25 AM. The scent came in waves of deliciously hot oat flour toasting in the oven. I blew through the door, zeroing in on the kitchen table. I had a one-track mind and an incinerator for a stomach. Mom, hair still in rollers and wearing a powder-blue bathrobe, had made my favorite breakfast: homemade bread, browned to perfection. She'd added local honey and a healthy dose of freshly ground peanut butter from the co-op: pure heaven.

With one thick slice down the hatch, I looked up at Miss Tease, my sister, Traci, suffering from mood poisoning. She wasn't digging the favored-son treatment. While my parents loved us equally, I received more than my fair share of attention. But focus and love were sometimes entirely different. Traci, far tougher than me in most regards, glared back. Her leg performed an anticipatory dance under the table. The usual signs were at play. She wanted a throwdown, an all-too-common occurrence in our house. I sighed, fighting the urge to slip into my role as Mr. Whine—another unfortunate but accurate family nickname.

Traci dished out an exaggerated eye roll, reminding me that teenage girls were, and forever remain, enigmas. "I'm still stronger than you," she jabbed to reorganize the family pecking order.

"Yeah, right," I said. "Game on."

We slid out of our chairs and raced to the living room before Mom could turn away from the stove. The shag carpet was our octagon, offering a sizable platform for the matchup. I tilted at the waist, assuming my fight position. Meanwhile, Traci, still physically dominant, paced in her lavender pajamas, ready to trounce me at the first misstep. And as usual, my mistake came quickly. I juked out of position. Before I blinked, Traci had me on the floor. With my arms pinned down, she readied her favorite torture tactic: the wad of death—the absolute worst.

She was an expert at hocking the nastiest loogies. Gathering them from her depths, she hung them over my head while straddling my sparrow-sized rib cage. Traci never spit the loogie onto my face, but the threat alone generated a shrill that unearthed Mr. Whine.

Right on cue, I shouted for my rescue. "Moooooommmm!" I screeched. "Traci's doing it again!" I grabbed Traci's long mop of reddish-brown locks like a rip cord. She retracted the wad of death and let out an equally ear-piercing shriek.

The kitchen faucet abruptly stopped, and sure enough, Mom emerged ringside. She'd end the near-weekly pattern of mismatched wrestling contests yet again.

"That's enough, you two," Mom said, still tired after a night of waiting tables. "I mean it, Traci. We all know you're stronger than Todd. Enough. And kiddo, for heaven's sake, let go of her hair."

With proper dynamics restored, Traci smirked. She released me from her death grip. Then she gloated all the way to her bedroom, whistling the theme song to *Charlie's Angels*. Meanwhile, I joined Mom back in the kitchen to devour the rest of breakfast in peace. I inhaled my third piece of toast and downed a quart of unpasteurized milk faster than water. Then I headed to my room to suit up. I sat on the bed, staring at my wall posters—Dr. J, Larry Bird, Michael Jackson, and Christie Brinkley—a motley crew of icons. I enjoyed our conversations; they were the best listeners in the house. It was better than bringing back my imaginary Timmy, who was formless and equally noncommunicative by this age.

"You have to come too," I insisted, pointing to Dr. J, sky-high and mid-dunk at the 1976 All-Star Game. "Pinkie promise."

Julius Erving didn't take his eyes off the rim. But Michael Jackson stared me down with a soul-penetrating gaze. Meanwhile, Christie looked completely unbothered by it all. She was sexy as hell with her sly smile and distracting boobs.

"Promise," I whispered, staring just as hard back at Michael, my face inches from the dark matter of his pupils.

I could've sworn his eyes narrowed. I took it as confirmation. My idols would watch as sure as the night sky had stars.

Marv burst into the room, ending my stare down.

"Come on, Red Rocket, it's time to go," he announced, toting his gym bag. If I didn't know better, I'd have thought he was off to work as the Los Angeles Rams conditioning coach. Mom would join us later—without Traci, who shrugged it off as she prepared for her invasion of the mall at Fashion Island.

Marv and I cruised in the VW, windows down, drawing in

the soothing morning breeze. But, breaking the calm, Marv's voice had the power of a wind gust. He rattled on about hand positioning and weight distribution the length of the drive. I didn't listen. The bright white of my jersey in the side-view mirror was too distracting. *I have to keep it this white forever*, I decided. *I look good, like a football player.* In reality, I was a fresh-faced beach kid sailing toward a blue-collar beating.

The pressure was on—as much as it can be at age nine. I felt a little queasy but fully alive as we parked in the rapidly filling lot. Orange slices tucked under my arm and electrolytes in tow, I was ready. My little heart pumped for action. I left Marv in the dust, joining my polished west side crew, as clean-cut as our jerseys. We made camp on a grassy knoll beyond the field. It was a preview to a Civil War battle, with my troop eyeing our competition from afar.

On a shorter but girthy hill stood a more dominant team from Orange, California, illuminated by the morning sun. Bigger and more rugged than our stringy crew, they wore notably well-worn jerseys with stain-checkered pants. I'd soon learn that these boys, with their oversized bodies and streetwise minds, didn't mess around and were itching to splatter a new infantry.

I donned my helmet to add a bit of size before the descent. The rest of the Cheyennes followed suit. We swallowed hard and took to the field for our warm-up. As we moved steadily closer to the competition, any remaining nerves settled. They looked tough but hadn't endured Marv's gauntlet since infancy. My accumulated mental strength set me apart. I didn't know it then, but it would become abundantly clear within the hour.

Crowded around the bench, we listened to Coach rifle off position assignments. Marv was within earshot. "Todd, you start at quarterback," he said, rattling off the rest of the offense. Conditioned to think offensively, I fixated on the word *quarterback*. I'd always imagined myself as a wide receiver, but this announcement brought a toothy grin to my face. I'd throw the ball, making sense out of the cacophony of movement. Despite my disorganized mind, almost everything was clear when it came to football.

Then came the pep talk I would internalize and later call upon throughout my career. Coach's expression turned from jovial to dead serious. "Boys, we are here to take the ground they stand on. It's that simple—it's an ancient philosophy that goes as deep as your cells. So, today, in front of your friends and families, don't hesitate. Go take that land!" our full-throated coach declared. Marv nodded. We erupted into nine-year-old battle cries, obnoxious screeching sounds meant to intimidate our opponents but that, more likely, merely deafened our parents.

I didn't necessarily understand the deeper meaning behind Coach's words, but his passion and conviction stuck with me. The message resonated years later. He'd nailed the essence of the game, which was rooted in my psyche and genetic makeup. It was all about taking what I felt was rightfully mine, one yard at a time. And sometimes, if I was really lucky, an entire field length.

Inspired by Coach's zeal, my youthful exuberance was at full throttle. I bolted onto the grassy field with my musket of an arm, surrounded by a fresh-legged regiment. We huddled up, and Coach called the play: "Twenty-two double out," he announced, lining up behind us. He crouched to our level to make eye contact. He needed to keep everyone focused on the task ahead.

Before I could forget, I nodded and parroted the play call to my clustered crew in a misshaped circle. "Twenty-two double out!" I reiterated, surges of energy firing through my spindly body.

Most of the offense was equally enthusiastic. But two distracted linemen found something more interesting in the grass: a massive beetle to kick back and forth. And our fullback was busy searching the sideline for his mom. He didn't want to start until he found his audience.

Coach snapped the rogue soldiers to attention while the rest of the offense nodded, helmets wobbly on their skinny necks. With the starting line now at full attention, we took our positions. We were wide-eyed recruits for the first battle sequence. At the snap of the ball, both receivers took off for ten yards. Then they pivoted toward the sidelines. I threw to the one who looked more open and watched the ball ungracefully wobble like a duck awkwardly flapping its wings. I stared, along with a distracted offensive line. The ball made clumsy contact with the wideout's elbow, a foot shy of the target. The ball, equally discombobulated, bounced off my teammate. It flew directly into the grass, resembling the casualty of a hunt. The domino effect didn't stop there. I was knocked off my feet, with gravity taking care of the rest. Orange's outside linebacker couldn't resist a late hit. Now I was face down in the grass, pounding my plum-sized fist on the ground—a JV performance by anyone's standard. I wouldn't make eye contact with Marv, not yet. I imagined his grimace.

"Okay—again, until we get it right," Coach said with gusto. I nodded, also itching for a do-over.

"Twenty-two double out!" I spoke with more confidence this time. I desperately wanted to get it right. But two of my teammates were busy stepping on each other's feet. And one of the receivers was about to join them.

Coach observed the unraveling. He acted fast, with skills reserved for the most talented youth coaches. "Guys, glory time!"

he declared as if he had ice cream sandwiches at the ready. "You got this—focus!"

My teammates snapped to attention with bobbling heads. The lineup formed, a mirror image of the last play. Once the whistle blew this time, though, I was dialed in. As the receivers pivoted, the offensive line offered good protection. I threw a soft touch pass to the same receiver. It was a clean spiral, landing perfectly into his pint-sized mitts. But instead of taking off running, the receiver stopped, raised his head, and registered the victory. With validation from the sideline and extra maternal encouragement, he took off running about as fast as a windup toy. He made it another ten yards, the Orange defense in steady pursuit. They caught up eventually, but it was a formidable advancement for our offense.

"Nice work, boys," Coach and Marv shouted in unison as we celebrated our first down.

"Now, let's change things up a bit," Coach explained as we rejoined the huddle. "Sammy, you move to quarterback, and Todd, you take his spot as lead blocker, got it?" Sammy and I nodded and slapped five. I was thrilled about the chance to slam into other kids. Anywhere else, this would earn me a trip to the principal's office.

"Sammy, call thirty-six sweep right," Coach instructed.

Sammy nodded but promptly forgot the number. "Thirty-something sweep right," he shouted in the knotted offensive pod, hoping we were dimly aware of the play. All amped up from our success on the second down, we nodded vigorously with unchecked certainty.

While Sammy didn't remember the play call, his guessing skills were on point. He handed the ball off to the running back.

Meanwhile, I served as the freckled advance team, clearing his path in a manner befitting my Red Rocket nickname. I propelled my fiery body into the upper chest of a barrel on the defensive line. But as soon as my head hit the man-child, an audible snap halted my progress. A piss-warm stream began flowing from my nostrils and down my chin. It didn't take more than another second for this tributary to turn into a river. Then I rose from the ground. Faces looked on in shock. I tilted my head to take in their view. It was a visual I would never unsee: my snow-white uniform resembled a butcher's apron with blood spreading like an estuary. My freshly laundered uniform was a perfectly pure white canvas for the nosebleed of the century.

I didn't cry out as Coach hustled over. He served as the makeshift medic, ready to assess the damage. As he removed my helmet and zeroed in on my nose, I caught Marv out of the corner of my eye. He sauntered up with an expression of amusement I knew all too well. He basked in the scene. His face divulged a tinge of pride: his son was tough as nails—nothing to worry about here.

"You okay?" Coach asked, alarmed by the crimson tide.

"Quarterback," Marv barked, hovering to the left of us.

Coach and I cranked our heads in unison. My ketchup-colored face bore a blank expression. Meanwhile, Coach resembled a disillusioned Southern Confederate stumbling on his words. "Wha ... What?" Coach asked, unable to process Marv's suggestion.

"Quarterback," Marv grunted. "He's fine. Put him back in at quarterback."

Coach paused for a solid two seconds, but he didn't resist. He knew arguing with Marv was akin to spitting into the oncoming wind. "All righty then, quarterback it is." Turning to me, he asked again, "You're okay, right?"

I nodded. "Yup, I'm fine," I whispered with DNA sprinkling off my lips like a misting fan. I really was okay. Like most nosebleeds, it looked far worse than it felt.

So it was decided. But the referee looked on skeptically while I fell in behind our center, who walked on toothpicks to avoid the mess. I called the play thirty-three double corners, all while colorful spittle bounced off the bars of my helmet. Then I settled into a body-wide calm. I felt an unexpected wisdom beyond my nine years of life. Everything was different this time. My hands connected with the ball as if it was meant to be in my possession. I stepped back and paused, waiting to launch a cannonball at the receiver motoring to the corner. I anticipated the time to meet his mark. Then I threw a gleaming, albeit bloody, spiral. It moved in slow motion—a gradual launch. Meanwhile, it shed blood, raining down sprinkles of me along its trajectory.

I stood in awe, stunned to discover my position and signature throw simultaneously. I'd never be known for throwing beautiful spirals. But my craftiness and catchable throws, with an accuracy reserved for lefties, would set me apart. While I was a bloody mess, I was also on cloud nine for the first time of many over the next two decades. Often retrieving this memory from the archives, I replicated this throw during USC's infamous win over UCLA in 1990. Minus the red mist, I threw the same beauty to Johnnie Morton in the end zone. It was a memorable final drive, leading USC to a 45–42 victory over our archrivals.

There was another reason this experience was formative to my development as an athlete. It offered an important lesson about not revealing weakness. Did my bludgeoned nose hurt in the moment? Sure, but it was temporary. The opposing team watched to see how I responded: Fold or fight? It told them everything they needed to know. Momentum would swiftly swing in their favor or rally my guys to fight harder for the win. Getting back up and pushing on was critical in that moment. Marv knew it, imparting his wisdom. So I discovered that football was not only physical but also overwhelmingly mental. It was a lesson I wouldn't forget.

Seventh-grade basketball reinforced the importance of my cerebral game. Some of my greatest sports memories are from my travel team. It helped that I had a fantastic coach, Gary McKnight. His technique and the players' talents combined to make a squad so good that we entered multiple tournaments most weekends. The games were often in different zip codes, so Coach would take half the team with him and send Marv with the rest. Marv was no basketball savant. He was the first to admit it. However, Coach had trained us so well that all Marv needed to do was make sure we got to the court on time.

What made Coach McKnight so great? He kept it simple. He was adamant about me knowing my role and executing within my capabilities. And when I forgot, he quickly reminded me with his booming voice: "Todd, you're in range when you step into the gym. Shoot the ball or get it to Tony. You got me?"

His instruction never wavered. I was a good shot with the confidence to make more than my fair share. And our power forward Tony Rocco was off-the-charts good—our Shaquille O'Neal. He was an absolute beast in the paint, a man before his time. While he was a teammate in basketball, the Italian Stallion was a rival in Little League. The mutual respect ran deep, and on-court success accelerated our growth. But it wasn't just Coach and Tony that made me a better player. I have the free throw line to thank for solidifying my mental fortitude.

It was a late-January weekend in 1981. I was off to Victoria Park in Central Los Angeles with Tony and five others. We headed north while Gary took the remaining seven south to San Diego for an equally compelling tourney.

The ride offered a visual lesson as we ventured out of our upper-middle-class Orange County bubble into Central Los Angeles. We traveled from well-appointed strip malls and car dealerships surrounded by smooth pavement to rows of shuttered stores, barred windows, and pocked, uneven streets. Once we entered the gym, I noticed that the players and fans were different too. First off, they didn't look like me. There wasn't a white guy among them. And it was crowded—the games were events not to be missed. While we filled half the bleachers at home, this place was jamming. Devotees weren't shy about showing their passion for their hometown boys. It brought a big smile to my face. This looked genuine, unlike the buttoned-up reserved claps from Orange County fans. I fed off the energy. Meanwhile, some of my teammates moved cautiously, as if they'd landed on Mars.

Once I took my eyes off the supporters, I checked the double doors to the gym. I could swear Shaft stood at the entrance where you'd typically find security. He greeted everyone in the neighborhood with smooth moves and elaborate handshakes. He wasn't the gatekeeper; he seemed more like the official greeter. With an untrained outside eye, it would be easy to confuse the two roles, but I saw it clearly in his embrace of all who entered.

As warm-ups started, a boom box blared funk rather than

our usual Bee Gees' "Stayin' Alive." My guys ran onto the gym floor more cautiously than lab rats. In contrast, the Victoria Park team sprang out of their locker room in sync with the beat. The band joined in, swinging their instruments and sliding along the bleachers. I came to a complete stop, in awe of the cinematic quality of the moment. The place was more vibrant than any movie I'd seen or imagined.

Shouts from the crowd picked up momentum at the jump ball. Tony faced off against Victoria Park's biggest guy, Willie. Our Italian didn't have a chance in hell. We nodded and took a defensive posture, dropping back from the circle to prepare for the onslaught. While these guys were a formidable challenge, we offered some excellent plays in return with fluid ball movement and a respectable outside shot percentage. I pulled in some solid numbers in the first half, and we started the last quarter neck and neck. Willie was gassed; it was apparent to everyone in the gym. This overgrown kid rested his hands on his knees every time the clock stopped. So I was less afraid to get the ball to Tony in the paint, where he could work his magic. As the last minute of regulation ran down, it remained a tit-for-tat battle from the three-point line to the paint.

Then, with thirty-five seconds on the clock, Victoria Park's wily guard tomahawked my shot and the rest of my body on a jumper just inside three-point range. I went to the foul line with the two most important points of the game on the line.

This was when I learned how to deal with pressure, solidifying my mental game. The gym was a disharmony of sounds that rattled through my mind. I looked over to Marv, who was silent. He observed my reaction with keen interest. Meanwhile, my teammates shouted words of encouragement. But they were muffled by my opponents, who slammed their hands along the bench.

The close score brought out the crowd's aggressive side. They chanted and booed as the referee threw a bounce pass to the foul line. He gave me the nod. My mind settled, blocking out much of the noise as I concentrated on the net. One bounce, two bounces, three, pause ... deep breath, a spin of the ball, and a bend of the knees. I took another deep breath to settle in and launched the ball. In my mind, I was alone in the driveway. No one could hear the swoosh but me. Again, boos from the crowd. I looked beyond the referee. I saw a few preteen girls shooting visual daggers my way. I smiled, registering the attention and turning it to my favor.

I reset and repeated my predictable foul shot pattern. One bounce, two bounces, three, pause ... deep breath, a spin of the ball, and a bend of the knees. Another deep breath, and *swoosh*. I was a shooting machine. Now we were up by two.

Victoria Park inbounded the ball. They made it down the court in time to nail one from the paint. But we weren't through. Our point guard found me in the corner along the three-point line. As I went for the shot, I was whacked again. Back to the foul line for another pressure-cooker moment. There were three chances this time, but sinking each one was necessary to take the lead. Winning the game was on my shoulders.

This time, the crowd was more openly hostile. It was difficult to ignore them on the first shot, since the noise was deafening. But my pre-shot ritual worked. I sunk the first one. The second shot was equally high-pressure because it would tie us. The ball circled the rim this time, debating whether to let gravity work in my favor. After licking the circumference twice, the ball dropped in, securing the tie. Now it was game on. I was full of anticipation. My next shot would secure the win. I ignored the fiery crowd, repeated my pre-shot ritual, and scored—nothing but net. We took home the win, and life taught me another lesson: I had what it took to triumph, regardless of the opponent, place, or crowd. It was within me, both innate and bred. I called upon this strength many times over the next two decades.

Free throw master.

While I succeeded early in football and basketball, track and field was another situation entirely. I hated it with a passion. But that didn't matter. Marv insisted on the sport because it helped my conditioning, mental strength, and overall toughness. He didn't care about the medals and accolades. He just wanted me to grow as an athlete and human. So I ran the grueling 400-meter race along with the long and high jump.

While I experienced some success in the field events, the 400-meter slog was my nemesis. The worst part was my overwhelming fear at the starting line. I became acutely aware of my isolation—raw and exposed. There was none of the camaraderie and comfort that accompanied team sports. My anxiety had eaten through any rational thought by the time the gun went off. And then there was the wall that I inevitably hit rounding the third corner. No matter how hard I trained, it was always there to greet me. Pushing through that corner made me stronger and introduced a powerful revelation: when my body said "enough," there was more gas in my tank every time.

By eighth grade, I couldn't take much more. I broached the touchy subject with Marv. "Do I have to do track in high school?" My eyes pleaded for a reprieve.

"No, Red Rocket. Once you get to high school, you choose," Marv said, already fully aware that it was not my sport. But it didn't matter; he'd just wanted me to experience adversity because it's an inevitable part of life. In hindsight, I'm grateful. Because of track in those early years, I grew stronger. I had greater command over my mind, at least when it came to sports. The rest of my life still presented formidable challenges, as I would battle negative self-talk for the foreseeable future.

While the track induced panic, baseball had the opposite effect. It put me to sleep. My journey started with T-ball in the park next to Balboa Pier and ended unceremoniously after eighth grade. Even the high-action pitching position left me bored. However, this didn't stop the Anaheim Angels from selecting me in 1988 in the forty-third round of the draft. It wasn't entirely out of left field, though. I was a known entity, having worked with one of the Angels' team doctors to improve my peripheral vision. I'd also visited summer training camp with Marv during junior high. Yet, even with the nod from the major leagues, my path was clear.

The gravitational pull of football was undeniable. Even Coach McKnight affirmed my path. He pulled me aside one day after practice at the end of seventh grade and unselfishly admitted, "Todd, football is your sport. Not basketball—football."

I nodded but continued with both sports. Gary's words only reinforced what Marv and I already knew. Whatever was not in my DNA was hard-packed through immersion every fall weekend of my childhood. The typical routine included Papa Fertig taking me to a high school football game on a Thursday or Friday night. I served as a ball boy for Edison High. Then the family set up camp at the Coliseum on Saturdays. My close-knit clan included former players, alumni, and an extended posse of die-hard Trojans. As if that wasn't enough, Rams games often dominated Sundays while Marv was their strength and conditioning coach. It was fair to say that I lived, breathed, and ate football each fall— and I loved every minute of it.

I remember precisely when and where I declared my passion for football. I was only ten years old. Marv was explaining something about my body alignment when I cut in midsentence, unable to contain my feelings any longer.

"I love it," I intervened. "Football."

"I can tell." Marv eyed me with his signature intensity. "If you're willing to spend the time, I know what it takes to succeed."

"Let's do it," I replied with the conviction of a ten-year-old. I was willing, but in hindsight, how could I have understood what I was signing up for? Well, it became apparent quickly. Gone were the days of aimlessly cruising the cul-de-sac. Movie nights with friends were increasingly rare—and forget about the monthly parade of birthday parties. At the infrequent celebrations I attended, I came with my own Marv-sanctioned cake and ice cream. The white devil, aka sugar, was rat poison in his eyes.

I was all in and raised the stakes by the end of seventh grade. I set the goal to be the first freshman in Mater Dei history to start at quarterback for the varsity team. Then I told teachers and whoever else would listen that I'd play in the NFL someday. This garnered plenty of polite smiles. A few suggested finding a backup plan.

I ignored the naysayers. The one opinion that mattered most was Marv's: he was in my corner, and it made all the difference. So, many years later, when the media suggested that Marv pushed me into football, I rolled my eyes and laughed. They couldn't have been more wrong. Football was the choice I made, plain and simple. If I'd chosen basketball or track, he would have stuck with me all the way too. But here's where it got tricky: Marv's commitment to my goals and experience in football unleashed a fervor not previously observed in youth sports.

What do I mean? I didn't make it through a full tackle football season until high school. Why? Marv bodychecked my coaches when he disagreed with their decisions. It sounds outlandish, I know. He got quite a reputation, but his passion, though sometimes misguided, was well intended. Never once did Marv put himself first or waver from my goals.

The year before high school was akin to working three jobs.

I had school, sports, and training. Marv posted goals in the dojo to keep me on track. The first was to weigh 175 pounds by high school. I barely met the target, given an insanely high caloric burn rate. The other objectives littering the garage were based on Marv's experience training varsity-level athletes. They included goals for deadlifts, cleans, the bench press, squats, forty-yard dash, and agility. Meeting these targets, regardless of my age, gave me the unequivocal confidence that I had what it took to make it at the varsity level.

Chapter Five

Marijuana-vich

Mater Dei High School's football training camp during the summer of 1984 was hell. It was also nothing like what I'd expected. Far from receiving an open-armed reception, I entered as a fifth stringer, fighting my way up the ranks. As far as the coaches and other players were concerned, I was just a wide-eyed, overeager freshman with pipe dreams.

Did I belong? I remembered Marv's goals in the garage. Numbers didn't lie. But building relationships and camaraderie hadn't been targets on the wall, so I was ill-equipped to navigate the favoritism of other quarterbacks who were long-standing teammates. Receivers stretched extra wide or fought for another step to secure a ball from their buddy. In contrast, they switched on autopilot and were a little less motivated during my reps. Nothing was worse than knowing that the ten guys in the huddle didn't want me to be the eleventh.

Despite the interpersonal challenges, more reps elevated my confidence. Meanwhile, the starting and second-string quarterbacks became increasingly concerned about their hold on the top spots. They simply couldn't match my touch, accuracy, and timing. By the end of hell week, it was apparent to the coaches and most of the team that my dream could become a reality. But when camp ended, I was left hanging on the ladder waiting for a final decision. Two days before the first game, Coach Chuck Gallo announced the starting lineup.

I would be the first freshman in Orange County history to begin the season at quarterback. Overwhelmed by the news, I couldn't wait to tell Marv. I caught a ride home and burst through the garage door to find him sitting at the kitchen table with Traci. "I'm starting at quarterback," I announced, eyes dancing as if it was CNN breaking news. Traci nodded, largely unfazed by the statement that had little effect on her world. In contrast, Marv leaned back, soaking in the moment of triumph. I watched the edges of his mouth curl into something loosely resembling a smile.

"I did it, Marv."

"Yup, you earned it, Orange." Marv didn't seem surprised. He wouldn't say he was proud, but I knew it. "That's what loading the wagon will get ya." Marv couldn't resist the opportunity to use one of his catchphrases. It was about as much celebration as I'd get out of him on a good day.

Someone else caught wind of Coach Gallo's decision: Stanford. The college's first temperature check came in the form of letters and promotional materials early that season. And once my face landed in the press, one of their assistant coaches started showing up at my games.

The national media attention, which focused on my upbringing and athletic prowess, forced me into the spotlight long before I was ready. I didn't even know myself yet. But at the vulnerable age of fifteen, the media painted the picture for me, truth be damned. It began when *People* magazine reached out to Marv to schedule an interview. A week later, the crew showed up at the house with a writer and photographer who acted more like detectives on the hunt. As soon as I caught sight of the camera, my stomach launched into acrobatics. I assumed Marv would hang close to manage the process, as in all other aspects of my young life. But just as the crew settled in, he pulled a Houdini, sliding into the adjoining room. Without media training or reinforcements in my corner, I was anxious, uneasy, and fully off-kilter for the next hour.

"Tell me how you got into football." The interviewer sensed my nerves and lobbed a softball to break the ice.

It didn't help. My stomach somersaulted as I stumbled over my words. It sounded like I was more frightened about football than in love with the sport. *Ugh.* I prayed for a course correction on the next question.

"Okay, tell me more about what you eat before you train with your dad."

Oh shit. I had to be careful answering this one. I rattled on about the things I ate at home, which excluded all processed foods. I sounded nothing like a typical teenager.

The interviewer raised his eyebrows. He'd caught the scent of blood. I had no idea he intended to go in for the kill as he nodded and walked me out on a plank.

I survived the next thirty minutes, but then came the photo shoot. Still awkward in my young skin, I couldn't get comfortable no matter what the photographer did. After another thirty minutes, he either got what he needed or simply gave up.

The issue arrived on the newsstands just as I'd purged the

ordeal from my short-term memory. Much to my surprise, I dug the pictures, along with bombshell Lynda Carter on the cover. Yet even though praise for my early performance was circulating widely, the article didn't focus on football at the private Catholic institution known for graduating future NFL stars. Instead, it made eye-catching claims about my diet, garnering an avalanche of attention. The coverage made me feel like a complete and utter freak show, not a star quarterback. It was hard enough with my flaming-red hair, heavily freckled cheeks, and sinewy body. I'd emerged from my prepubescent stage with scarcely a hair on my nuts. Now, I was a media-manufactured Frankenstein. I was mortified, dodging any mention of the profile piece in the hallways and locker room. With that kind of coverage, fitting in with the older, more developed guys on the varsity team would be an uphill battle.

There was a complicating factor to this early attention: I was partly to blame for the media pile-on. Beginning with the *People* article, I went along with the party line about not eating junk food—never a Big Mac and the like. It wasn't because I wanted to lie. Far from it, I needed to avoid Marv's wrath. Deviating from his strict diet plan was a serious no-no. But in reality, Mom and her family let me eat all kinds of things throughout my childhood. My favorites were the doughnuts that I forever associated with Papa. We would cruise to the shop on Balboa Peninsula in his golf cart on many Saturday mornings to scarf treats swimming in white-devil glaze. Marv never knew, and no one fessed up. So the charade continued, and the media didn't dig for the truth. Satisfied with their storyline, they sold sensationalism faster than candy.

But I was ill-prepared for more than just the media. My

Spartan-like existence changed abruptly with the introduction of weekly postgame keggers. Being a socially awkward freshman, I lived in perpetual fear during these outings. *What if they think I'm a dork?* If I had any chance of leading these guys on the field, I needed respect off the turf too. So I dug deep and struggled to blend in with the crowd.

Fear hit me harder than a medicine ball at a house party early in my first season at Mater Dei. After trouncing our competition, I entered a vast vaulted entryway of a magazine-worthy beach house. Standing outside the living room, I watched an animated, alcohol-fueled game of quarters. I hadn't even stepped foot in the room and was already an outsider. The guys looked cocksure, standing wide and secure. And the smokeshow blondes seemed more like women than teenagers. This was nothing like my handful of eighth-grade backyard sleepovers.

"What the fuck, Todd—get in here," a lineman taunted.

"Yeah, come on." Another teammate tossed a quarter in my direction. His perfectly stacked girlfriend eyed me skeptically. I was little-brother material, not a serious prospect.

"I'm coming," I said, mustering some flimsy confidence. I took a second to steady myself. With my throw and accuracy, it might be my game. *How bad could it be?* That thought always got me into trouble.

I joined in, initially bouncing the quarters with a fair bit of success. After ten more minutes, I blended into the group of upperclassmen and breathed a sigh of relief. Then it was my turn to down the beer—not my first, but the inaugural one at a high school party. I tilted my head back and chugged it like water. Then I felt a quarter hit the back of my throat. *Oh shit.* I panicked and swallowed hard, feeling the weight of the metal careen to my stomach. *Fuck. How am I going to play this one off? The next person looking for the quarter will figure out what I did.*

Sure enough, less than a minute later, a sandy-haired cheerleader with nothing better to do outed me.

"Ewww, gross, you just swallowed it!" she announced loud enough for everyone to hear. I'd heard plenty about these mean girls; they were a dime a dozen at Mater Dei.

"That's just weird, man," the usually fly-on-the-wall punter blurted out.

"Yeah, what the fuck?" a benchwarmer piled on. He was fondling the babe on his arm, who stuck to him like an octopus. While he wasn't a starter, landing a hot chick meant he had plenty of street cred.

I wanted to shrivel into a raisin. My face glowed a rainbow of reds, and a raging river of panic flooded my body. I instinctively reached for a half-finished Budweiser. And not just one—I guzzled as many as I could get my hands on that night. "Another round," I declared to get the next game in motion.

From then on, I threw drinks down my gullet before parties to avoid another mishap. If I entered with a strong buzz, I was less likely to blow my cover. It was a relief to take all the fear out of the equation. And so, at age fifteen, I became an alcoholic. Fear and booze were my gateway drugs.

By the end of my freshman season, I had set my priorities: partying and football, in that order. Gatherings were memorable if the team played well and won, but I focused on living it up beyond the turf. That meant a steady stream of alcohol. I strived for the six-beer buzz but hated the associated bloating. That's when I migrated to liquor. The hard stuff relaxed me fast with less discomfort—a double win.

Then one of my favorite receivers cracked the door to something far more alluring.

"Have you ever tried one of these?" His face was obscured by a cloud of smoke after a postgame party in Dana Point.

"No," I responded, wide-eyed and eager. The war on drugs raged, and I was beyond curious.

"I think you'll like it." He passed me a joint nearly the size of a hot dog.

Never having seen one up close, I took it between my fingers. It certainly didn't look dangerous. I pulled in a drag and held it for a few seconds. It felt as natural as breathing. Within minutes, all the stress melted away.

I wanted more. This was the feeling that had eluded me for years. For anyone else, it might not be addictive. In my case, it was a critical lifeline, easing me through the socially complex bubble known as high school. The weed quieted nagging negative self-talk, ushered in relaxation, and unleashed a more popular version of me. *Who was I, really?* Like many high school kids, I sensed my true identity was still a mystery. However, unlike most of my peers, I would need several more decades to assemble the puzzle.

While I drank and got high at Mater Dei, my football experience went by in a flash. Despite my off-field antics, I threw for 4,358 yards and 34 touchdowns in two seasons. I had the perfect setup with great receivers, including Mike Mitchell. He was the prototype wide receiver of the future: a multitalented stud who could leap out of this world. Despite missing the season's first five games, he still led the country in receiving. Any time I doubted where to throw the ball, I sent it high in his general direction, a long ball that looked like it was orbiting Earth. Mike always caught it. After a few games with his surefire mitts, my confidence spiked.

The media continued to put me on a pedestal throughout the rest of high school. It reached a crescendo in 1987 when *California* magazine labeled me the "Robo Quarterback" with a large spread. While Marv was thrilled, I was mortified. Marv and the media wanted me to stick out, but I just wanted to fit in. I loathed my portrayal as an oddity once again as the media grossly distorted my existence. *Why does everyone always think of me as a freak show?*

The ensuing pressure was untenable. They also painted Marv as a fanatic, which was only partially true. Remember, I wanted it—but what was "it" exactly? I wanted to be a football standout, not a circus act. Like Mom, I voiced my concerns to Marv that things were out of control. It fell on deaf ears: he insisted that the attention was necessary for my ascent to greatness. He had no true sense of the cost that would come in time.

Then, before my junior year, everything changed. I abruptly transferred to Capo: Capistrano Valley High School. Marv pulled the rip cord fast that summer, sharing the news over dinner while Mom was still at work. I didn't protest openly. It would be useless. The loss of friendships hard won over the prior two years wouldn't concern him. Instead, I moved food around my plate, waiting for the chance to escape to my room. I kept my emotions bottled up in his presence. Things were easier that way.

In my room that night, I worried about making my mark at Capo, my future, and mainly about Mom. *Where does she fit into this new equation? Does she even know?* I barely slept that night, holding on to porous truths: Marv had my best interest at heart. And all I wanted to do was play football at the highest level. I repeated these beliefs until the words faded from conscious thought.

Later, I learned that Marv had completely abandoned Mom, not informing her about the move. She had enough once she saw it in the newspaper, which cited their marital separation as an excuse for the change in schools. Since their acrimony was public, it was time to end their failing marriage after twenty-four years. However, as part of the deal, I moved in with Marv and left Mom in Newport Beach. In that swift move with little notice, I lost my foundation and the buffer that had counteracted Marv's extreme tendencies for my first sixteen years. While Mom mourned the loss, like me, she had no choice but to accept her new reality.

Now Marv was in charge with no emergency brake within reach as we careened down the hill. We were in a new town with an entirely fresh existence. Marv was a bachelor for the first time in his adult life while I was a budding addict. The situation had hazard written all over it. It was increasingly dangerous for me: being at public school meant that I didn't need to stay on campus during lunch breaks—the perfect excuse to get high. Within months, I was toking before school during zero period, between classes, and even before practice. I was no longer dabbling on the edges of addiction; I was jumping in headfirst.

My only abstinence was on game days, mostly so I wouldn't get caught. I didn't want to upset one of the most influential coaches, Dick Enright, for many reasons. I respected his talents, learned from his wisdom, and lived in his house. Well, not exactly his home. It was more of a partitioned in-law suite where Marv and I took up residence when we jumped from Mater Dei. Was it a violation of the California Interscholastic Federation (CIF) rules? Hell yeah, a transfer living with a head coach looked terrible on paper. But it was the perfect situation. In contrast to Mater Dei's pint-sized coach, Coach Enright led with a wealth of experience. He was a beast of a man—a former offensive lineman for the Los Angeles Rams. He'd even groomed another one of my quarterback heroes at Oregon, Dan Fouts. This signal-caller went on to lead the San Diego Chargers.

While I had taken too many hits and bent several knee braces at Mater Dei under a self-professed offensive guru, I learned about complex football under Coach Enright. What were his secrets? It was the football version of Maslow's hierarchy. Safety and security came first. I evaluated our vulnerabilities, scheme, and line protection, so I was less jumpy. With this baseline of confidence, I could focus on getting the ball to the open guy. Coach Enright also taught me to read and anticipate a defense. I studied my opponent's coverage diligently, identifying their tells. Once I knew their tendencies, basic math skills came in handy. Within a second of handling the ball, I ran calculations to expose the opponents' position of weakness.

Yet even with all this preparation, it wasn't a smooth start at Capo. In my first game against Foothill, I broke the tip of my left thumb. Since it was my throwing hand, Marv escorted me to the emergency room for a rapid-fire assessment before returning to the game. Despite the clubbed thumb, I managed to throw for 122 yards, including two touchdowns in the final eight and a half minutes. It was quite a rally, but not enough to overtake our opponents; we came up short with a final score of 28–26.

With the freak accident in the rearview mirror, I settled in for two heavy-growth years under Coach's superior instruction. Consequently, I experienced remarkable progress, breaking the all-time Orange County passing record and later the national high school record, passing for 9,914 yards, including 2,477 in my senior year.

But beyond the favorable blocking and pass routes at Capo, my partying went unchecked. Public exposure to my growing addiction hit harder than a two-by-four during an infamous basketball game in my junior year. I was at the foul line against the El Toro Chargers, preparing for my first shot, when the crowd started to chant. At first, I didn't pay attention. It sounded like my last name, but my mind was in the backyard shooting baskets. After I sank the first shot, I paid closer attention. They weren't shouting my last name, not exactly. It was worse . . . far worse. In sync with the bleacher foot stomping, they belted out "Marijuana-vich," more relentlessly than a washer stuck on a spin cycle.

I panicked, searching for Marv and then Mom in the crowd. Of course, they were there, on opposite ends of the bleachers. They heard the chant as clear as day. Marv was expressionless, his well-worked arms crossed in his tracksuit, staring straight at me. Mom's face contorted as her watery eyes jumped like a ping-pong ball from me to Marv and then back to the crowd. After the game, I prepared for the riot act that never came. They wanted to push it under the rug as much as I did. So we buried it deep into the fibers, never to be excavated.

While my parents didn't want to bring it up, the fans sure did. Word spread faster than breaking news around the league about Marijuana-vich, the stoner. Yet remarkably, it never hit the press.

Just when I thought I was in the clear, someone else, almost as important to me as my parents, had his way of tackling my growing reputation: Coach Enright. Football season had ended months ago. Marv and I had moved out of the in-law suite, instead sharing a tight, bare-bones apartment near town, with me in the bedroom and Marv on the couch. Yet even with the increased distance from Coach, I found my way to his doorstep on weekends to help in the yard. On one occasion, he broached the subject of my drug use with an unexpected gentleness. It surfaced family wounds involving a son who'd suffered from addiction and lost his college scholarship.

"Todd, I don't know much about addiction," he stammered, clearly distraught as he bent to grab a rake. "But . . ." He paused a long while. "I love . . . actually, I am addicted to cheese." His eyes, so large and earnest, didn't blink. He leaned in as if he'd confessed the ultimate sin.

I stared back at him, perplexed and too curious to let it die on the vine. So I encouraged him: "Ummm hmmmm, cheese." I nodded to coax him along.

"Yeah, I love it, kiddo. I can't imagine not eating it," he admitted.

My mind danced with wacky images, including Coach as the world's most oversized mouse, eyes gleaming as he spotted a heavy wedge of Swiss cheese. He'd drag it away and gorge on this pocked block of day-old dairy.

Coach Dick Enright.

Coach stammered, realizing that his analogy was bizarre at best. "I'm just saying that I understand how hard it is to stop. I couldn't resist cheese if you made me." Then he resumed his raking.

I examined his expression, bemused by the comparison. He was so genuine and worthy of connection at that moment, but I couldn't open up. This was simply a blip on my wild, twisted journey. I convinced myself that no one understood and stuck by this conviction. No one really knew what it felt like to want to escape yourself. That's what I believed until joining like minds in rehab.

Coach's attempted inroad was the only one I recall from high school. Others were focused on awards and my future. I finished out the year with a slew of honors, including Parade All-American, the National High School Coaches Association's Offensive Player of the Year, Dial's National High School Scholar-Athlete of the Year, and the Touchdown Club's National High School Player of the Year. All this fanfare meant plenty of cool trips with different family members, from Mom and Traci to Papa and, finally, Marv. It was one long party where I met sports legends while gathering a chest of awards. As for Marv, he downplayed it all. In his view, it was simply a by-product of putting in the work. "Just keep loading the wagon," he reminded me.

While these honors applied a candy coating to my high school career, the Marinovich household was abuzz about the next step in my journey: Where would I go to college? Mom was partial to Stanford. Papa bled cardinal and gold. Uncle Craig, who was intimately associated with USC's program as a star quarterback and assistant coach, reinforced the gravitational pull of the Trojans. Meanwhile, Marv, believe it or not, didn't offer an opinion. Unlike in my first eighteen years of life, when he displayed zero self-restraint, he wouldn't offer up one piece of advice. Crickets. Nothing. He wouldn't budge. This marked a turning point in our relationship. In his eyes, I was no longer a child. Everything from here on out was my decision as the master of my destiny.

I knew one thing: I wanted to be on the West Coast. And I wasn't shy about sharing it with anyone who asked, which narrowed the field. In my eyes, this meant Stanford or USC. The rest of the schools, and there were plenty, were background noise.

Instead of launching a pressure campaign, Papa, always the voice of reason, asked a straightforward question one night after dinner: "Where do you want to live after college?"

I didn't hesitate. "Southern California, of course."

With that, four years of heavy recruitment by the widely respected Jack Elway, John's father, at Stanford was for naught. I was going to USC to win a Rose Bowl. I imagined it well before it happened.

But despite my conviction, I still agreed to one deviation: a recruiting trip to the University of Miami. They were national champ contenders in the late 1980s. I was in their crosshairs, given my high school record and national recognition.

Jimmy Johnson, who later coached the Dallas Cowboys, led the charge. It all started rather innocently. Jimmy's office asked about my interests and wooed me with calls and flashy promotional materials. Then they designed a dream-worthy recruiting trip, enlisting their star wide receiver Michael Irvin and arranging a visit to a reggae festival.

But first, I had to stop through Washington, DC, for a stuffy award banquet. It was a boring night until Mom, Traci, and I discovered some entertainment at a stopover on our ride to the hotel. Dressed to impress, we traipsed through Georgetown to check out a few watering holes. At our third stop, I looked back at the staircase to the Tombs just in time to watch Mom, always dressed to impress, stumbling. Down the stairs she went with her hat askew and fresh holes in her pantyhose. Consistently a lightweight, Mom was definitely lit.

The following day, Traci dragged Mom to the Smithsonian. Meanwhile, I would head to the airport for my Miami recruiting trip. I woke up hungover, remembering the endless pitchers of beer. I checked the clock. The last place I wanted to go was to Miami to tour a football program. Hell no, I wanted to go home—as in, my bed, home. But, hit with a wave of obligation, I called a cab and headed out on Route 66 toward Dulles Airport. Halfway there, I panicked. I couldn't find the plane ticket. I rifled through my duffel bag in a nauseated state. *Fuck, I left the ticket at the hotel.* There was only one explanation, or so I thought: *divine intervention.* The cabbie found a rare off-ramp, and we cruised back to the hotel. Mom and Traci piled into the room an hour later, chipper and chatting until they eyed me on the couch.

"Todd, what? Aren't you? Miami?" Mom stumbled on her words.

"I'm not going," I announced with zero hesitation. The gods were with me on this one. "Look, you know I want to stay on the West Coast. This trip would be a waste for everyone. I won't end up at Miami; there's no chance."

"Well, the least you can do is call and let them know," Traci stated, always the most responsible of the bunch.

Mom fished in her purse and found the number for Miami's athletic department. I left a message politely informing them of the change in plans. Then, as expected of a short-sighted kid, I promptly forgot the whole ordeal. That was until I was on the runway for my Los Angeles–bound flight.

The plane pulled away from the gate—nothing eventful. Then it taxied toward the runway before it came to an abrupt stop. "Todd Marinovich, please come to the front of the plane," an authoritative voice boomed over the loudspeaker. Mom bolted upright in her seat and looked at me. Then Traci craned her neck around Mom like a bug-eyed ostrich, mouthing, "What the fuck?"

I shrugged, unbuckled my safety belt, and slunk up the aisle to the first-class flight attendant. "There's a call for you. We're turning around and heading back to the gate so you can take it." She tried her best to be polite, but her tight pink lips and frosty tone revealed her growing frustration. Some rat-haired redhead had thrown off their schedule. She'd kick me under the plane if she could get away with it.

"Ummm, okay," I responded cautiously. "Should I go back to my seat now?"

"No, stay next to me in the jump seat so you can deplane quickly." She took her seat, overcaffeinated and jumpy as I slid in next to her.

All the passengers stared at me. *Back to a freak show on public display. Fabulous.* I needed a drink.

I disembarked and approached the gate, where another attendant handed me a phone.

"Todd?"

It was Coach Jimmy Johnson. *Oh shit, this isn't good.*

"Yes, hi, Coach Johnson." I tried to sound casual, as if this were no big deal.

"Todd, I just got word that you aren't joining us this weekend." He sounded surprised.

"That's right, Coach. I've decided to go to school on the West Coast."

"Well, I want you to know what you'd be giving up before you make that decision, son." He cleared his throat and continued, "You know we don't recruit kids from the West Coast. Wanna know why?" He didn't wait for a response. "Because we don't need to. We're one of the best, if not the best, program in the country." He paused for effect. "We only want the most elite athletes in our program. We see that in you."

"Thank you, Coach. I appreciate your vote of confidence. But as hard as this is to say, I have to stay true to my heart. I belong on the West Coast. I'm so sorry."

The supremely confident Jimmy Johnson wasn't below one last appeal. "Okay, son, but if you change your mind, you know where to find me."

"Thank you, Coach. I sincerely apologize for the last-minute change. You've been nothing but gracious. I'll always remember that."

"All right, Todd, off you go." Coach Johnson hung up the phone, forever a gentleman but wise enough to recognize a lost cause.

I was honest on the call, though. There wasn't a chance in hell that I'd ever forget that a plane had been rerouted back to the gate so I could talk with a football coach, never in a million years.

So I took the show on the road in 1988, up the 405 Freeway to USC, nestled in South Central Los Angeles. I'd rub elbows with everyone from the privileged to gangbangers in one strange cauldron of colliding worlds. It looked like heaven from my vantage point, though. I had a free ride, and I'd make the most of my time there—on and off the Bermuda grass.

Chapter Six

High Functioning or Functioning High? My USC Days

I arrived on USC's campus naively believing I was free from the shackles of a manufactured identity. Yet I soon realized my media reputation as a squeaky-clean kid was a headwind. Classmates and teammates assumed I lived more strictly than a monk, treating my body as a temple like the national coverage suggested. With the student body from across the country arriving on campus well before the advent of social media, they hadn't been privy to the chanting student section at Capo High, which never made the news. So jaws dropped when they discovered a fatty in my mouth at campus keggers and lines of coke in the bathroom. Forget about no sugar or artificial preservatives; few chemicals were off-limits, especially if they ushered in instant gratification. But there were plenty of restrictions on my budding freedom, including football and addiction. I couldn't escape 2 PM daily practices or silence the inescapable urge to get blitzed. Both were full-time jobs; eventually, one would have to give. No one, including me, expected football to end first.

My redshirt year allowed me to observe, learn, and salivate. I had twelve months of practicing against one of the best defenses in the country, including powerhouse lineman and team captain Tim Ryan, who went on to play for the Bears, and inside linebacker Scott Ross, who later joined the Saints. And then there was the beloved and infamous Junior Seau; he was an absolute beast in college and then in the pros with the Chargers, Dolphins, and Patriots. This was not a shabby defensive line by any measure.

Of all the 1988 starters, the kind and jovial Junior was the only familiar face. Back in high school, I scrimmaged Ocean View High. He was the lean quarterback with a basketball physique. By college, he'd packed on a solid fifty pounds, and he came so hard out of the corner, with a high-pitched Native American chant, that it put any quarterback on edge. After several practices, I had to warn him: he gave away his signature moves with all the racket. From then on, he attacked as silently and lethally as an assassin.

Junior and I also spent plenty of time together off the field, including at a Samoan wedding in Carson, California. I was the only non-islander in attendance. The ceremony was in the couple's native language, so Junior whispered the play-by-play for over an hour. That's just who he was: a humble-hearted guy who wanted everyone to feel accepted. So he gave love and received a ton in return.

That was true of most of the team, though. It was a tight-knit band of brothers. I vividly remember one early showdown against Oklahoma. Any lingering uncertainty about my USC decision vanished as I emerged from the tunnel in a sheath of goose bumps beside some of my favorite teammates: Tim, Scott, and Junior. Instead of the maximum of ten thousand in attendance at my biggest high school games, roughly eighty thousand fans were packed into the stands. My insides screamed, *This is where I'm meant to be: with my boys, suited up in cardinal and gold.*

The Coliseum was a legendary spot to call home—where every Trojan since 1923 had played the game. It was also the site of two Olympics, two Super Bowls, and even the World Series. But more importantly, it was the Marinovich family church: sacred ground where our clan had worshipped for generations. It was a legacy that I carried with pride.

After the warm-ups, I found a spot hovering just out of view of Coach Larry Smith but still within earshot. He was relatively new to the Trojans, in his second year leading the team. We had little in common since he was defense oriented and a no-nonsense guy. He also seemed pretty decisive, bordering on rigid. Perhaps his brief stint at West Point was to blame, or a more fundamental personal code of conduct that didn't tolerate deviation or deviants? It was clear from the start that we weren't on the same wavelength. Yet clicking with a coach was a desire, not a necessity for success. And so, I watched and learned as he dictated orders from his razor-wire-thin lips.

After the first whistle blew, the show began, an experience like no other as the players executed Coach's finely tuned commands. Every fiber of my being wanted to be on that field. It was college football at its best. I watched teammates having the time of their lives. Quarterback Rodney Peete grinned from ear to ear while the undersized Scott Ross, a wild-eyed terror, repeatedly blew up plays. Scott capped these victories with his signature celebration move: straight-arm guitar circles directed at the crowd. The Coliseum ignited every time. During a TV time-out, he found Matt Gee and me, another newbie, to fire us up even more. "Watch this next move," he said, flashing a high-beam smile. Sure enough, he rocked the house again in the next series.

Matt and I ribbed each other and hollered. Inseparable that season, we were the only two young guys on the road with the team. It was not expressed but implied: we were the team's future leaders. Matt was a solid guy from Kansas who I admired for many reasons, but mainly because he possessed what had eluded me for nearly a lifetime: he was comfortable in his skin. Although he had a purple birthmark on half of his body, he never tried to hide it, or himself, for that matter.

After nearly all the home games, Matt and many other teammates would meet at the California Pizza and Pasta Co., also known as the 502 Club, which we all called the Five-O for short. It earned this moniker in the 1970s after nose tackle Rich Dimler's drunk driving citation number. Known for its sports crowd, it sat within throwing distance from my dorm, Heritage Hall. Despite being so close, however, it was far out of reach. The bouncer, Vance, deflected my attempts to enter. I didn't understand: other freshmen gained entry without issue, but not me. After several failed efforts, I concluded that the owner, Tony, had something against me.

I boldly approached him on my way to an afternoon class late in the fall.

"I'm Todd," I offered, extending my arm for a handshake.

"Ah, yes, I know who you are," Tony said, grabbing my mitt.

"Did I do something to upset you?" I asked gently.

He examined my face, squinting in the glaring afternoon sun. "What do you mean?"

"I've noticed plenty of other freshmen in the Five-O, but I'm refused every time," I said, a bit flustered, my cheeks getting warm.

"Yeah, they're not Todd Marinovich," he stated, raising his eyebrows and pointing at my chest. He paused, looked around, and stepped closer. "Look, kid, I'd love to have you in there, but you are a lightning rod... too visible... too known."

"But all my teammates are there after the games."

He looked me straight in the eye and truly saw me: someone who just wanted to fit in. His face softened.

He sighed and looked around again, contemplating his options. "Give it two more games. After that, Vance will let you in. But we want to avoid any heat for an underage phenom boozing it up, got me?" he said with the heart of a compassionate ex-athlete colliding with the mind of a practical business owner.

"I won't do anything stupid, I promise," I insisted, hoping it was true. I'd do my best.

A man of his word, Tony granted me passage after another two games—both wins. Like any carrot held just beyond reach, it looked far sweeter than it tasted.

Not long after gaining entry, an incident at the Five-O influenced the rest of my career. I sat with Matt, wolfing down half a deep-dish meat lover's pizza, a pitcher of beer between us. We replayed moments from the game that had ended a mere two hours ago. We'd give a kidney in exchange for game time, but it wasn't in the cards for two redshirts.

Tim Ryan waved us over as I wiped the pizza grease from my mug. "The big man is requesting us," I informed Matt, gesturing in Tim's direction.

Matt smiled. "Oh shit, what now?" he joked. Tim was one

of the nicest guys on the team but not a force to ignore. At 270 pounds, this slab of grade A sirloin unleashed hell from the defensive line.

We approached the bar. Tim handed us each a fresh beer before launching into his speech. "All right, guys, listen up. You've heard the news about the drug test coming up, right?"

Word had spread through the locker room in less than a minute during pregame practice. It was a rumor but not far-fetched. Tim's concern meant it was imminent.

"Yup," Matt and I said in unison. Matt looked unconcerned, so I followed his lead. While he was judicious in his pot smoking, I was anything but conservative. As for the rest of the team, plenty of guys partook, but I'll take those names to the grave.

"Well, it's time for you to learn three very important rules." Tim's face was deadpan. He wasn't fucking around. I tuned in and sat down, a student at the most important lecture. Matt, a formidable linebacker in his own right, blocked lingering attention from other patrons. He spread wide, placing his beer on the bar.

"Okay, guys."

We leaned in.

"No matter what happens, you must . . ." Tim paused for effect. "You must . . . deny, deny, deny."

I nodded; it seemed simple enough. I looked at Matt, and he cracked a smile.

"No, guys, really. This is serious shit. You must always deny, deny, deny, no matter what." Tim looked stone-cold sober; his pupils were dilated with a schoolboy's earnest expression.

Then it dawned on me. The guys knew I was a big smoker, swallowed my share of ecstasy, and sniffed more than a few lines.

The risk of guilt by association was too great for Tim, Scott, and many other players. They'd fall into the rabbit hole with me if I went down. Their careers and potential futures in the NFL were on the line. No matter how much they liked me, they wouldn't let some redshirt freshman put them in jeopardy.

"It's the only rule. Actually, it's our golden rule," Tim announced with bucketloads of conviction.

"Our golden rule. You got it," I parroted back. And that it was. I lived by the tenet for decades, denying any allegation within striking distance.

Despite the off-field activities, we ended the 1988 season with a solid record of ten wins and two losses, going eight and zero in our conference. Winning the Pac-10 championship was well deserved and only slightly stained by our loss to Michigan in the Rose Bowl. Sometimes you can't have it all, but we certainly got close.

As the football season ended, the widely respected basketball coach George Raveling approached me about joining the team. While it was an honor, I couldn't imagine balancing two sports with partying.

"You saw me play in the CIF championship, yeah?" I asked.

"You bet. You've got a lot of talent. We could use your accuracy from the outside."

"What about Harold Miner?" I questioned. He was their star, nicknamed Baby Jordan because of his jaw-dropping skill. "There aren't enough basketballs on the court for me and Harold," I kidded.

"We could find a way if you're interested," George explained, throwing out the proverbial temperature check.

"Thanks, Coach, but I will take it all in from the bleachers. My hands are full with football."

George stared off, nodding. "Yeah, I figured, but you can't blame me for trying."

While I didn't seriously consider the offer, I felt validated. I'd spent just as much time in the gym as on the field over the prior decade. As I stood there with Coach, a long-tucked-away feeling reemerged: a different kind of freedom discovered on the court. When I played hoops, I didn't have a single worry. There was no pressure to perform because it was my second sport. But something else made me feel liberated too: alcohol and drugs. I wasn't about to clock in for another four months of physical stress and strain when I could be doing keg stands and lines of coke.

Before the start of the 1989 season, the team went full throttle, and I got tossed into the blender. I never saw it coming. I stood behind Pat O'Hara, who had a cannon of an arm. I waited for my reps when I saw the collision and heard the sickening pop of Pat's knee. Everything moved in slow motion as teammates surrounded the star quarterback with expressions of dread. I joined them, in shock over the severity of his injury but also my new reality. I'd get my chance to lead, but at the expense of another teammate. It was not how I wanted my story to unfold.

Consequently, I became the first freshman quarterback to kick off the season for USC since World War II. Much to everyone's surprise, it turned into one hell of a ride. It was so good that buttons appeared around campus reading, "In Todd We Trust." No pressure. It turns out that my arm and accuracy, combined with poise in the pocket, led to very good things. By the end of it, I was named the Pac-10 Freshman of the Year; I'd completed 197 of 321 passes, scored 16 touchdowns, and had a healthy 61.4 completion percentage during the regular season.

The 1989 season.

The year came with its share of trials, though, especially after losing the season opener to Illinois by a measly point. Then I started my first away game, our conference opener, with the wind at my back on a cold September day in Pullman, Washington. It had dropped thirty degrees overnight when we entered the outdoor meat locker. To add insult to injury, the field was Astrocrete, meaning it was so fricking hard that it was basically cement painted green. The perks kept coming.

While Washington State hoped to pull out an upset, we were jacked from the start—perhaps a bit too confident. They managed to upend our passing game and kept us on our heels. Our offense couldn't be counted out when it mattered, though. We secured our first touchdown in the second quarter to set the tone. It didn't take long for a strong response from the Cougars to tie the game. Everyone seemed to pay attention to the defenses on both sides while we botched our offensive opportunities and racked up penalties.

It was 17–10 favoring Washington State in the third quarter. Then I threw a frozen rope to John Jackson, who gave it the tiptoe to keep both feet in. A few minutes later, I lost my shoe in a scramble. Somehow, I kept advancing on one wheel. I felt a semitruck bearing down on me, but I didn't give up. A few plays later, I looked over to see Coach smiling, a rare occurrence. We were down, but he sensed what I knew: we were about to do something great.

I led a last-minute comeback known as "the Drive." It was a ninety-one-yard battle downfield, without a single running play or time-out and several fourth downs to keep everyone gripping their seats. Then I hit the versatile and quick running back Ricky Ervins on a flat route for a touchdown. The guy was a magician with the ball, darting through the defense, a controlled and compact rocket at five feet seven inches. Now anything was possible.

Again, I looked over to Coach, who was still smiling. It was time to go for two. I was ready. I called the same play and held on to the ball. Like Joe Montana in "The Catch," I lost some ground while trying to buy time. I pumped, pivoted, and felt a growing tightness in my chest. I didn't have much time to make it happen. At five feet nine inches, Gary Wellman was no Dwight Clark, but he was my guy. Gary was deep in the end zone, almost on the line. *Oh shit, stay inside.* I threw and time stood still. The ball connected with Gary as the defense collapsed on him. I watched him on his tiptoes, wiggling to ensure they were still in. *Hell yes, they were inside the line.* We won the game. It was Mardi Gras and Christmas all in one.

The crowd went silent, quieter than a morgue. The turn of events crushed them. The quiet allowed me to fully absorb our away game celebration as guys hollered and pounced into a pileup on Gary like kids into a mound of leaves. The whole team lingered on the field to absorb the priceless riches of our work. While some teammates glorified Gary, others launched me into the air like it was the Second Coming. This victory was special already, but the unimpeded bonding separated it from all others. The win signaled the start of something extraordinary that year, and we all sensed it.

We were still celebrating back in Los Angeles when I was summoned to Coach's office for a phone call. Right away, I knew something was up. I racked my brain on the short walk. Sure, I'd partied hard after the win, but I'd kept it reasonably clean by an addict's standards. My senses were on high alert as Coach's secretary gave me the nod to enter the office. I sat across the desk from an empty throne and waited, with the tick of the wall clock as my sterile companion. Then the secretary cracked the door.

"Pick up line one, Todd," she said, her eyes eager for me to act.

I gingerly brought the phone to my ear. "Hello?"

No greeting, just a mechanical order from an operator: "Please hold for the president of the United States."

What. The. Hell. I gulped air as I coughed on saliva, never having imagined this situation.

Then the leader of the free world greeted me with a casual "Hello, son."

"Hi, Mr. President," I said awkwardly, as if I was a serf and he was my king.

"I saw your performance in the Washington State game. I was in the hospital, laid up after a minor procedure when I caught that game-winning drive. It was one of the best executions I've ever seen."

"Thank you, sir. It was a moment I'll never forget."

"You and plenty of college football fans too." He paused. I heard papers shuffle. I wondered if he was home from the hospital, making this call from the Oval Office or the West Wing.

"Well, if you're ever in the area, in Santa Barbara, that is, I've got a little ranch there," he said, trailing off as something in the background seemed to distract him. *Maybe Mikhail Gorbachev was calling on the other line about the Cold War? Or was Nancy telling him to close out his night?*

"Yes, I've heard about your spread up north. Does it have a pool or a pond?"

"Both, but the pond's probably better for you," he decided.

Ah, yes, more suitable for a serf, I thought. "Probably so. Thank you, Mr. President. I hope to take you up on that someday." I left off the last thought racing through my mind. *Maybe I can get some time with Nancy while I'm there to talk about that "just say no" nonsense?*

I never made it to the president's ranch, but it was an excellent way to wrap up a near-perfect week.

The momentum seemed to be in our favor. We were in solid contention for the Pac-10 championship. But outside our conference, there were a few setbacks, namely Notre Dame on October 21, 1989, in South Bend, Indiana. The Fighting Irish ranked first in the country. They had no intention of ending their eighteen-game winning streak. Their sights were on a national championship, but we'd do our best to throw a monkey wrench into their plans.

First, we needed to make it past the pregame. That

shouldn't have been a challenge, but the Irish designed it to be a struggle. They positioned themselves between us and our tunnel. This meant threading through a seam, dropping a shoulder if necessary, or finding a way around them. There was no good option.

On cue at the close of the pregame warm-up, Notre Dame's hefty reserve guys started lining up along the end zone. I thought nothing of it, weaving through without a problem before they'd fully formed the line. I headed to the locker room along with a few backs and receivers to wait for the rest of the team. I sat and stared at the clock, but no one showed up. After water and a bathroom break to kill time, my concern mounted. Then the guys straggled in with bloody noses and the early signs of black eyes. Even our security guard, Xavier Suazo, whom everyone called X-Man, was a wreck. This former special agent, short but sturdy, staggered in with a puffy lip and missing eyetooth. I was thunderstruck: this stud had spent a career dealing with criminals. Whatever had happened on the field was bad. Very bad.

"What the heck, X-Man? You okay?" I asked, my mouth agape.

"That was some crazy-ass shit out there," he said, wiping blood from his upper lip with his forearm. "How'd you make it through the end zone without a scratch?"

"I was ahead of you guys. What'd I miss?" I sought some reasonable explanation for the steady flow of injuries.

"They wouldn't let us past the goal line. They jumped us, three guys to our one. With those kind of numbers, we ate shit." He fought to catch his breath. "A straight-up brawl in fucking South Bend," X-Man said, still in disbelief.

"Where's Coach Smith?" I wondered aloud.

X-Man shrugged his shoulders as he assessed the damage to his mouth.

Seconds later, a fuming Coach burst into the locker room. He looked okay physically, but he was about to flip his lid. Flanking him were a few assistants with torn shirts, so I realized the Irish had targeted our coaching staff too—pure insanity.

Coach called everyone to attention. The place looked more like an ER waiting area than a locker room. "What just happened out there is outrageous. No matter the outcome today, I want you to take it to them on the field." He threw down his clipboard, red-faced, nearly begging us to fight back. He didn't have to plead. We frothed at the chance to right the pregame wrongs.

Charging out of the locker room, we were motivated, equipped warriors. It worked, at least for the first twenty minutes. We held a 17–7 lead going into the second half. But despite our best efforts, including John Jackson's fourteen catches, Notre Dame's quarterback Tony Rice scored a late rushing touchdown. The Irish inched us out 28–24. When asked by reporters about my efforts that day, I could only remark, "Not good enough to win." It killed me. I wanted to finish what the Irish had started, but it wasn't meant to be.

Later that season came "the Granddaddy of Them All," the 1990 Rose Bowl that fulfilled a childhood dream. We matched up again with Michigan, who had beaten us the prior year 22–14. We weren't about to repeat history, but many bet against us given Michigan's regular season record of 9–2. Michigan was ranked seventh in the nation. As for us, we were on their heels with a 9–2–1 record, placing us eighth.

Sequestered for the week before the game, we stayed in familiar territory: a hotel at Fashion Island in Newport Beach. We practiced at the University of California, Irvine, in the fields where USC held camp every summer. The week was pretty uneventful until a small group of us went on a caper before the coaches could tighten the screws. I gathered my inner circle, including Tim Ryan, Matt Gee, and Matt Butkus—yes, the son of the NFL great Dick Butkus—along with a few other rebels.

The Red Onion, a local hot spot, had neared capacity when we arrived. I found a seat at the end of the bar and ordered my customary beer with a shot of Jack Daniel's. About two rounds in, I noticed some guys our age and size enter. Then I looked closer. Yup, it was a few like-minded Michigan players. *Crazy coincidence, what are the odds?* Matt Gee noticed them, too, and looked back at me. We hatched the same plan simultaneously; I could tell by his sneaky kid-in-the-candy-store expression.

"Fuck it, why not?" I blurted out.

"This should be interesting," Matt whispered, waving the Wolverines over to our end of the bar. This caught Tim Ryan's attention as he shook his head and laughed. Our behavior would surely become part of Trojan lore.

The competition didn't hesitate. The first guy I met was offensive lineman Greg Skrepenak, who became a fellow Raider years later.

"Hey guys, guess we all got sick of the endless routine," he said, donning a wide grin as he flagged the bartender.

"Yeah, the coaches would shit seeing this," Matt Butkus weighed in. He had less on the line, with fewer minutes despite his pedigree. He was a lukewarm player but shined off the field. A true comedian with a lovable personality, Matt was one of my closest friends at USC.

"No game talk." I raised my second round of Jack.

"Hell no," two Wolverines agreed, beers in hand.

By this point, my tolerance was off the charts. I could go toe to toe with the Clydesdale-sized linemen, ordering my signature beer and Jack shot twofer. The only telltale sign of my buzz was my brazen confidence with women, which was nonexistent sober. But while at the bar, my competition was more than entertaining. They were guys I'd hang with at USC: fun and up for a party. Despite the adventure, I was restless when I returned to the hotel and rejoined my roommate, quarterback Shane Foley. I was on the prowl for more fun. Just as I resigned myself to bed, there was a knock.

A classmate was at the door. I immediately scanned her plump lips, form-fitting T-shirt, and tight jeans—*cute and convenient, double win*. I'd noticed her before but never given her a serious thought. She was a mainstay at all the games and had a reputation for enjoying the players. I guess it was my turn at the wheel. Undoubtedly fed up with my less-than-model behavior, Shane rolled over and covered his head. Meanwhile, I guided my guest to the bathroom. We didn't speak a word until the door closed.

"Just checking on you," she whispered, making quick work of my T-shirt.

"A thorough check," I remarked, hoping I'd remembered to brush my teeth. She didn't seem to mind, as her pace accelerated.

"Fair is fair." I pulled off her T-shirt, exposing a sheer, lacy bra.

I unbuttoned her jeans with one hand while turning on the shower. It turns out that Marv's efforts to make me ambidextrous came in handy in many aspects of life; go figure. I just wanted to drown out the noise, but then she slipped off her jeans and moved into the shower. She went commando. *My kind of girl*.

"I'm game." I dropped my shorts and joined her. As I navigated her body like a Slip 'N Slide, she turned her back to me and offered the universal signal: a gentle hip thrust in my direction.

It was my go-to position until, mid-thrust, I got a little too enthusiastic and slipped out. On the return, I made a fateful error straight into the nether region. *Oh no.*

Her head rotated like Linda Blair's in *The Exorcist*. She let out a squeal that probably stirred Shane along with half the hallway. "Todd, I thought you had accuracy!" She didn't hold back.

I just about died. I was speechless. I smiled, acting as if it was all part of the plan. But in reality, it was far from it. Many of my crew were into this geographic deviation, but it wasn't my thing. That said, I didn't relocate the football. My buzz gave me the confidence to venture into new lands—a landscape where I was one and done.

By the morning of the Rose Bowl, my cup had runneth over. The week had offered more relaxation and preparation than any coach could provide. And fortunately for me, my unsanctioned activities had gone undetected.

I took the field for warm-ups and committed the scene to memory as a feast for the eyes with vivid primary colors. Our white uniforms, my favorites, contrasted Michigan's stunning dark blue, and a bright-red painted rose graced the middle of a field of rich, green grass. While my visual senses lit up, my ears got a shock right before the game. We were in the locker room, preparing to head to the tunnel, when I heard a thundering boom and the place rattled. *An earthquake? A bomb?* It was a sound so unfamiliar that all I could imagine was war. It wasn't until we ventured out onto the field that I learned the Blue Angels had streaked by at low altitude. Now that I was on high alert, my fight reflex entered the mix. I was ready to play.

Despite the lead-up, the game itself wasn't a stunner. It was, however, an excellent defensive battle. We gained the advantage in the first half when I ran for a one-yard touchdown. It was actually a mistake. I turned the wrong way and missed the handoff, but I saw the opening and ran like hell. By halftime, Michigan had only picked up three points with a nineteen-yard field goal. But things changed in the third quarter as the Wolverines tied things up with Allen Jefferson's two-yard run and J.D. Carlson's kick.

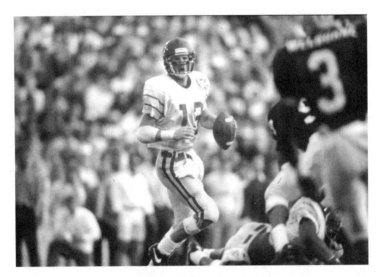

The 1990 Rose Bowl.

Then came the fourth-quarter clash. Coach Bo Schembechler surprised everyone with a fake punt. Next, Chris Stapleton took twenty-four yards only to be called for holding. We were sweating it, but Ricky Ervins ultimately gave us the win with a fourteen-yard run into the end zone to punish Michigan. It was a hard-fought 17–10 victory.

Smelling the roses.

At the end of the game, Schembechler refused interview requests and retired after twenty-one years of Michigan coaching. Meanwhile, I had no idea of the magnitude of the Rose Bowl win for Coach Smith. His relationship with Schembechler dated back to Bowling Green, followed by Michigan, where he'd served as an assistant. He had beaten his mentor, every protégé's dream.

Given how things were unfolding, what could go wrong? Famous last words. Although my dreams had come true, my USC unraveling was imminent. Even though I was a Heisman candidate, it was a rough 1990 season, especially my relationship with Coach. I had the invincible attitude of a twenty-one-year-old, which led to nonstop head-butting against the guy who ran the team as an army. Things got explosive fast. He'd yank me in and out of games at the drop of a hat. I'd even sit out some trips when we could handily thrash a team. Then, out of nowhere, *USA Today* suggested that I was considering a move to the pros. It was kerosene on a brush fire.

The smoke was a cloud over the season while the heat of the fire came for Coach. Those in the know understood an uncomfortable reality: his success in the prior two seasons had been primarily due to Ted Tollner's recruits, not his. What do people often do when they feel threatened and backed into a corner? Ah yes, find a scapegoat, and fast. I seemed like a great one. Unlike in the prior two years, he zeroed in on classroom attendance.

Word got around that I was skipping lectures more frequently, so Coach threw his penalty: more games from the bench. Then he called me to his office for the umpteenth time that season. I braced myself for another lecture. He didn't beat around the bush. "Why the heck do you keep missing class?"

I heard the echoes of my teammates: deny, deny, deny. It seemed logical to apply this to all situations with potential consequences. I looked up from the floor and met Coach's eyes. He looked genuinely concerned, something I never expected given the state of our relationship.

"I hate school," I admitted, risking some of myself with the unvarnished truth.

"Well, if you could do anything, what would it be?"

"Art." The word tumbled out of me.

"Then that's what you should do," he said with the tone of a parent.

I envisioned Marv's raised eyebrows and soul-piercing look of disapproval. I explained that Marv didn't want me to become a starving artist, so it was a nonstarter. Coach's permission, though, stated more like an insistent father, set me free to pursue my passion.

The change in my major from geography—taking a page from Michael Jordan's playbook—to fine arts altered everything. I found my people. However, I couldn't join the studio classes because of the practice schedule, so my professor gave me a key to work in the evenings as a compromise. My creative juices flowed late into the night. It felt heavenly to sit with one of my lawless creations. It took me back to Newport Elementary School, where art class flew by in seconds.

But the warming ground between Coach and I returned to permafrost soon enough. Once again, I was back in his office, eyes glued to the floor.

"Here we go, another round," Coach said with a sigh.

Good, at least he remembered our last treaty.

"I got a report of two guys up to no good. One was six foot four with fiery-red hair, and the other had a sizable birthmark. Sounds strikingly familiar, don't you think? If I were a betting man, I'd put my money on you and Matt Gee." He paused for an awkwardly long moment to let me stew.

Deny, deny, deny. "No chance, Coach. I was in bed," I stated plainly. *Shit, wait, he hadn't said when—a fricking trap.*

"Don't you want to know what night we're discussing here?"

Shit. "It doesn't matter, Coach, I haven't done anything wrong." That was all he'd get out of me. I was fed up with his sources, suspicion, and need for a fall guy. No matter what I did, I'd end up back in this chair. *Why bother even trying to fall in line?* Coach would find something. He had to find something.

Sure enough, a few games later, he fixated on everyone wearing shoes and keeping their hair cut. *Was this football or the army?* Now I was confused and obstinate. I wore flip-flops everywhere but on the field. And my hair? Well, it was part of my persona: wild as hell. He was targeting me yet again.

While hair was a sore subject for me, it was the source of attention for another teammate. I was dying to take a leak at halftime during one matchup at the Coliseum. I beelined it into the locker room, irritated that I had to remove all my gear. As I rounded the corner to the sinks, I came within feet of tight end Patrick Muldoon—yes, the future actor—pressed up against the ledge to get a closer look in the mirror while blow-drying his locks. No fricking joke. He saw my jaw drop, laughed, and made some comment about looking good for the hot chicks in the stands. Once the rest of the team filed in, I couldn't resist the opportunity to deliver a memorable ribbing. That's what teammates do, tease the shit out of each other. As much as I poked fun, I appreciated the aura of playing at USC with its beautiful campus and students. If there was ever a place for a future actor to play football, USC made more sense than any other college, except maybe a few of our subsequent opponents.

To no one's surprise, Coach left me behind for the next game against Arizona State. Then came our home matchup against Cal. I went from deflated to gutted. While I started, it didn't take long to get pulled by Coach. He was up to the same old tricks, behaving worse than an on-again, off-again girlfriend.

After a series, I relieved Shane Foley. Then my hometown crowd, who'd loved me for the last year, began to boo. Not quietly, mind you—as loud as hell for the longest jog from the sideline to the huddle. And there was no confusion about the target of their ire. The commotion started precisely when I took the field. Word must have traveled that I was on Coach's shit list. I was in a daze, in complete shock, and deeply hurt by the kiss-and-kick nature of these fans. Tears welled in my eyes as I looked down to regain my composure. Lineman Pat Harlow snapped me out of it. He frothed, spit, and screamed in the huddle. "They're booing our boy," he shouted, incredulous.

Calling the play was difficult. I barely kept myself together.

Maybe it was the gods taking pity on me, but somehow I threw a touchdown on the next play. Yet the crowd had extinguished my flame—my love for the game. It took all my energy to walk off the field, weighed down by something close to physical pain in my heart.

Pat, on the other hand, was still riled up. He leaped to the bench and faced the student section. Waiting for their full attention, he offered them the double middle-finger salute. Knowing my brothers had my back was a reprieve from the pain. I didn't realize until later that my whole clan, both Fertig and Marinovich, had dealt with their own melee in the stands. The Fertig line—Papa, Gramma, my uncle, cousin, and Mom—engaged in a war of words with vicious fans. But that was nothing compared to the Marinovich side. Marv and Traci weren't just shooting verbal daggers—they threw punches. Both of them were forcibly restrained and removed from the Marinovich pews for mixing it up with nasty fans.

I appreciated the support from those closest to me, but the whole controversy my sophomore year was mostly my own doing or undoing. Decades later, I made amends. I reconnected with Coach's wife, Cheryl, and their son, Corby, in Arizona as part of the ninth step to recovery. While Coach had long since passed, his daughter, Ali, facilitated the meeting with the rest of the clan.

Cheryl shared much about the man behind the rigid persona. It turns out he was more human than I imagined. He was riddled with self-doubt, primarily as a result of our caustic dynamic. I was shocked by how much he'd shared with his wife. Then she offered a bittersweet final insight: one of Coach's greatest regrets was the disintegration of our relationship. I was floored.

But in 1990, there was no seeing the future—even the next day, for that matter. In the lead-up to the UCLA game, I was on alert while Coach remained tight-lipped. Then, with only six hours of notice after the prolonged period of indecision, Coach reluctantly announced that I would start. So much for mental preparation.

I embraced the silver lining: the chance to beat UCLA at home was irresistible. Two years prior, I'd watched this same matchup from the sideline with my uncle and cousin. In the closing minutes, we left our seats for a closer view. Walking from the UCLA sideline to USC's, we captured the final drive. Unbeknownst to us, the *LA Times* memorialized the moment. The family outing was in clear view, pasted on the front of the sports section the next day. It didn't take long for USC to get in some hot water for our mistake. As a recruit, I wasn't supposed to be on the sideline more than once that year. But getting that close to the action was an overwhelming temptation. Eventually, the heat blew over, yet the moment of victory lodged deep in my mind.

Fast-forward two years and exchange Rodney Peete for me: I was ready to repeat history. It was a game finish to savor forever. Both sides scored twenty-one points in the fourth quarter. In the closing minutes we needed a touchdown to pull off the win. Coach called a time-out. When the offense huddled up, he shocked us all: "What do you want to run?" he asked, looking directly at me.

Seriously? The man who had little more than a mustard seed of faith in me was handing me the baton for the last chance to pull out a win. The about-face was shocking. I waited for my guys to look up as I pretended not to hear over the crowd. I caught it perfectly but wanted my teammates to absorb his words. Our leader, the man with all the answers, was at a loss.

It was the final sixteen seconds. The pressure was on, but it didn't faze me one bit. These were my moments. I knew exactly what play I wanted to run: a carbon copy of my bloody spiral in my first tackle football scrimmage at age nine.

At the snap, I dropped back to buy time. I pointed at the corner to bait the defense and Johnnie Morton shook his head. Then I looked to my actual target, Gary Wellman, to see him pressed and jammed. So I toggled back to Johnnie, a restless freshman with only one touchdown so far that season. Like most receivers, he relentlessly begged for the ball. Now he had his second chance of the game—it was time to deliver. He made his move with a race to the corner. Johnnie had the safety beat, but he needed to backpedal.

Meanwhile, center Craig Gibson made a pass possible. He managed to get one hand on a stunting defensive tackle. Craig redirected him just enough to allow me to rip it. Confident that the safety wouldn't be a factor, I cocked and threw.

With the ball an inch or two out of my hands, I was lambasted by the defense. Falling to the ground, I watched Johnnie secure the ball for the win. I rolled to my side, registering a sea of cardinal helmets. Then a pair of Easter-egg-yellow polyester pants obstructed my view. Uncle Craig was on the field shaking me and shouting, "You did it, motherfucker! You did it!"

Chapter Seven

The Fucking Sun Bowl?

We fell short my sophomore season and didn't make it to the Rose Bowl. Instead, Coach decided to take us to the Sun Bowl in Texas over the Aloha Bowl in Hawaii. What the hell was he smoking? None of us understood his decision or actions leading up to the game.

He spent the latter part of the season mistreating many of us. Players who'd contributed to the Rose Bowl win the year prior were managed like deadweight as they dealt with injuries. *How can he sweep aside guys without respect for their contributions or sacrifices? Does he even care?* My animosity was off the charts. Finding a teammate in Coach's corner was a tall order.

Mexican tequila numbed my frustrations during the lead-up to the bowl game. I experienced the worst hangover of my life a mere three days before the main event. There was no sugarcoating—it was straight-up alcohol poisoning. I don't remember the bar or much about the Wednesday night before the game. Most accounts placed me across the border in Juárez, Mexico, which made sense given my vague memory of a border crossing. After that, I only recall the dizzying number of empty shot glasses on the sticky bar, the filth of the floor, and a brawl. The chaos commenced when some stranger rifled off a mouthful of shit about my deficiencies as a quarterback. I hadn't even lifted a finger before one of my guys cold-cocked him. This linebacker was always primed for a dogfight, especially when someone came for his own.

His action mobilized the masses, turning the place into a mosh pit of mayhem. Pushing and shoving rapidly escalated to throwing chairs and bottles. The night wouldn't end well at this rate. We had to move fast to evade the Federales, or worse, the local drug cartels. My last memory from the ordeal was being extracted by the lineman from the pandemonium and hightailing it back to the hotel.

I woke up in a puddle of vomit, praying I was back stateside. Then I crawled to the bathroom, hoisting myself to look in the mirror. My face seemed okay; my teammates had gotten me out of there just in time. But that's all I knew for sure. I froze with the unenviable urge to puke my brains out as the tequila and my stomach acid started to dance the salsa. I peered back at the bedroom clock. It was thirty minutes until practice, and there was no phoning in sick. I pulled on my clothes, grabbed my bag, and prayed for a miracle during the bus ride to the facility.

Calling plays in this condition was more challenging than designing a rocket ship. I couldn't even don my helmet without flinching. I lifted the cumbersome cage and squeezed it over my head, which pulsed with every graze against my skin. If I didn't know better, I'd have guessed an aneurysm was on the horizon. Absolutely nothing eased the ache in my skull throughout a practice in which time stood still—frozen like the brutal El Paso weather. Somehow, I managed to keep a low profile. I limped through the day, a quarter of my former self.

By that night, I was convinced that my head would split in half. When I thought it couldn't get any worse, waves of putrid air began streaming in the windows. It took me a while to figure out that it was burning tires from across the border. I couldn't escape the stench. By the middle of the night, I'd vowed never to return to El Paso—a commitment I've kept for thirty-five years and counting.

My head finally healed, and on the morning of the game, this California boy trudged through the snow to the stadium in flip-flops. The matchup was a full-on defensive battle—a slog of slogs against Michigan State. The score was a measly 7–6 for most of the game. And it wasn't my best performance—not surprising given the brain cells annihilated only days before. By the fourth quarter, the coaching staff had seen enough. Offensive line coach John Matsko, a barrel of a man, delivered the news: "We're going to go with Shane."

I glared at him, sparks practically flying out of my eyes.

Shane didn't deliver in the next series, so John rolled back my way. "When we get the ball, are you ready to go?"

I hesitated, sick of being jerked around. It wasn't what the coaches wanted to see. Coach Smith caught my body language out of the corner of his eye.

He approached, bringing a shitload of hostile energy my way. He unloaded years of suppressed frustration in under thirty seconds. I held steady without answering. "So are you going back in?" he half asked and half told me through his grimace. "I want an answer, damn it."

I looked at him and then at our bench of offensive linemen, receivers, and running backs and paused. "I'll go in for these guys." I pointed to the bench.

There was no stepping back from that steep of a ledge.

Coach lost his shit with hostility holding court. Full-on zero to sixty in a school zone, almost a Marv-worthy melt-up. I made out the bulging of his jugular as he radiated heat faster than a furnace in overdrive. I understood instantly that our relationship was irreparable. I never went back in that game because our opponents ran out the clock, but I meant what I said.

Not only was my imminent departure set in motion that day, but the team was in shambles after the one-point loss, 17–16. Then things really spun out of control in the locker room. It started when the running back coach Clarence Shelmon sauntered up to Shane's locker, which was adjacent to mine. He cleared his throat and aired his views to Shane so all could hear: "We should've gone with you the whole game."

I looked up, roiling. But I wasn't the only one. Clarence had no idea that he'd awoken the Kraken. Scott, a full row of lockers away, barreled toward him, tackling Clarence and pasting him to the ground. Bedlam ensued, a straight-up street fight as players and coaches locked collars and exchanged expletives in the sacred space. Thank god the season was over. Everyone needed time to get their temperature under control. As for me, I didn't cool off; I just took off—for the pros.

After the melee in the locker room, I called Marv from a pay phone outside the stadium.

I didn't even bother with a hello. "What a shit show," I said, exasperated.

"You can say that again," Marv stated dryly.

I began to tell him about the locker room fight, but he cut in. "Guess who caught your exchange with Coach?"

"What do you mean?" I wasn't following.

"ESPN, that's who. Everyone watching *SportsCenter* got to read your lips."

I paused, rewinding the clock to the verbal dress-down and my reaction. *Oh shit, I really said aloud, "That's it, I'm outta here."*

"Oh no," I said.

"Oh yes," Marv insisted.

I swallowed hard. My life was about to change, and the future was uncertain. I hung up the phone with a steady stream of concerns flowing through my head.

In hindsight, I should've worked through the tension with Coach for the sake of my teammates. Instead, I abandoned my brothers. It took another twenty years for those guys to come back into my life. I didn't realize then what I know now: the Trojan family was, and still is, real. And the sacrifices were sometimes fatal. Chronic traumatic encephalopathy (CTE) ravaged good buddies like Scott Ross, Matt Gee, and Junior Seau. Five of the dozen linebackers from the 1989 team died before age fifty. That's more than a coincidence, but I'll get to that issue soon enough.

These buddies didn't vanish from my thoughts, though. Memories of my time with them lived on. When I thought about Scott, crazy stories flooded my mind. A great guy most of the time, he was known for his itchy trigger finger. Usually it was consequence-free, but not always. I recall Scott punching a guy in front of his off-campus house, only to have gangbangers spray the place with a shower of bullets the next night. Remarkably, no one got hurt, but Scott never hit one of those guys again.

I also thought of Buster the Rottweiler. Scott and Buster

shared steroids, meaning Scott frequently put some of his stash in Buster's kibble. The man and beast went forehead to forehead, growling over leftovers. At first, it was amusing to watch. But over time, Buster's noggin grew to the size of a lion's head.

Along with Buster's increasing girth came an unpredictable temper. So my biggest fear wasn't stray bullets; it was stepping over Buster en route to piss in the middle of the night. A mere graze of his leg could result in bloody payback.

After several months, Buster hit the streets, stopping by less often for his steroid-laced chow. Then we received word that he had found a new home. He was the lead of a pack roaming South Central Los Angeles. I can only imagine the havoc he wreaked in backyards and alleyways as he transformed into the canine equivalent of Denzel Washington in *The Equalizer*. God save the 'hood.

Technically, I never lived in the Craftsman house shared by Scott, Steve Mills, and Gene Fruge, but their couch was form-fitted to my body. The quaint 1930s-style abode was a respite from life on campus, but the street was practically a war zone. It wasn't uncommon to hear automatic weapons fire at night and even, occasionally, during the day. Life was pretty colorful on that crazy street, and we only added to the palette.

As for racial distinctions in football, they never crossed my mind because I wasn't trained to think that way. The Trojans were a brotherhood with a common mission more compelling than any superficial differences. We fought for each other, not against one another; our fellowship was pure of heart.

Why entertain artificial divisions when we're 99.9 percent genetically identical? I soon discovered that this line of thinking wasn't shared by everyone. I recall a summer game in the Coliseum when ex-Trojans joined for a post-match party. I was in the locker room standing beside a guy who'd played in the 1960s. He'd heard stories about on-field tension between Scott Ross and tailback Aaron Emanuel. It wasn't racial; their conflict was an undeniable personality mismatch. But that didn't stop the alum from weighing in. "I see that things haven't changed," he commented, shaking his head as he filled his red Solo cup at the keg. I was about to defend Scott but caught myself. The words would fall on deaf ears.

The alum's comment stuck with me and emerged from the catacombs one pregame evening later that season. As was customary for home games, we stayed in a hotel in the Wilshire district of Los Angeles. It was also tradition to take two buses to Paramount Studios to watch a pre-release film in their plush theaters. I was late, so I jumped on the second bus in line. I stumbled up the stairs and noticed all the players staring back at me. Except for the driver, I was the only white guy on the bus. The realization that we naturally self-segregated, even in 1990, hit me hard. There was no excuse, but I know that it wasn't intentional. It was a disappointing habit, a mindless repeat of tragic history that had become so second nature that no one noticed until I broke the mold.

"Todd, you're on the wrong bus," someone shouted from the back. It sounded like Aaron, but I couldn't be sure. I laughed and took a seat close to the driver—some inexcusable habits die hard.

Then came Halloween, always an excellent opportunity to challenge identities, or more simply, justify another party at the off-campus pad. Given my artistic talents, I was in high demand during the lead-up. I painted Scott and Matt's faces like members of Kiss while they dressed as WWE wrestlers, donning huge wigs and shredded muscle shirts—believable enough to win prize money at the Five-O. Not to be outdone, defensive lineman

Dan Owens strolled in with my practice jersey, a red wig, and a joint you'd expect to see in Bob Marley's mouth. From a guy as straitlaced as Dan O, it garnered plenty of laughter. And my on-campus roommate, Jeff Peace, and I dressed party appropriately as Cheech & Chong.

Jeff was a blood brother, a guy always in my corner. Our connection went back to high school when I played against Mission Viejo. It was a frustrating game for me because this pain-in-the-ass middle linebacker kept blowing up plays. He was so single-minded that he foiled my chance at a South Coast League championship. I still broke the passing record, but this fucker made my night miserable.

The next day, I woke feeling like I'd aged fifty years. Everything ached.

"That guy got to you," Marv remarked as I stepped gingerly into the kitchen to make my morning shake.

"Yeah, he was a force." I was still irritated about the crumbling of a championship dream.

"Reminds me of someone I know." He wasn't letting it go.

I knew what he meant. That middle linebacker was a young Marv and my worst nightmare. I never wanted to see that guy again. I loaded the blender and let it rip to drown out Marv. Those few seconds gave me time to park the image of that pallet of C-4 behind the center.

The cacophony stopped, and Marv jumped in right on cue. "You're gonna call him."

I rolled my eyes. "No way. I don't even know his name," I fired back. It was the only deflection within my arsenal.

"You'll find it. Call that guy to congratulate him," Marv demanded as he walked out of the kitchen.

I knew when I faced a losing battle. It was time to wave the flag.

"Okay, okay," I grumbled, rifling through the cupboards for the honey.

I finally tracked down Jeff's information and called to get Marv off my back.

I still wanted to hate the guy, but much to my surprise, he handled the conversation like a champ. Within a few hours, we met up at the beach. It was the start of a lifelong friendship.

By Christmas, Jeff was on my back about colleges. He was heading to USC to play football.

"If you choose the Trojans, we'd be teammates and roommates," he reminded me. "And if you go to Stanford, we'll kick your ass every year. You sure you want that?" he questioned. "Remember that last game when I blew up all your plays? Well, get ready for that on repeat."

I knew Jeff was right, but I had to decide on my own. As soon as I did, we were inseparable. We were among USC's biggest recruits, Fluor Tower bound.

Everything fell into place, except for one unfortunate curveball neither of us could anticipate. Years of hitting caught up with Jeff at USC. He had tackled his way to a severe neck injury and was deemed medically ineligible. It killed him to watch from the sideline, but nothing could fix this terrible twist of fate.

Chapter Eight

A Renegade Gone Awry

Everything happened far too soon when I joined the NFL. Signing with the Raiders, once a dream, became a nightmare. It should've been perfect. Every comfort from home was within reach. But that was precisely the problem. I had my dealers on speed dial and a long-standing entourage sniffing out parties. Plus, I had access to plenty of cash with a $1 million signing bonus and a $2.25 million three-year contract. But my day job was anything but a cakewalk, so the balancing act was precarious at best.

I was no longer a standout on a roster loaded with Hall of Famers. Owner Al Davis, known for acquiring guys late in their careers, gave legends another stint to capitalize on their greatness. Strong safety Ronnie Lott, who joined the team my rookie year, was the perfect example. The guy was so dedicated to football that he amputated his fricking fingertip to avoid missing game time. He also garnered a bucketload of respect. He could stop practice on a dime to demand a repeat of a play. No one questioned him, not even the coaches. He continued his dominance and leadership off the field, regularly holding court during team meetings. Out of all the talent on the team, he was my greatest teacher. He showed me how to read defensive backs' body language, fake coverages, and other tells.

There were also plenty of former USC stars on the team, including Roger Craig, Riki Ellison, Don Mosebar, and Marcus Allen, whom I admired more than the rest. He moved like a cat on one play and then blocked with the best of them on the next. No other running back did more to support his team than Marcus. As a result, every Raider, except maybe the owner, would take a bullet for him. And he's the only player I've ever seen get a standing ovation from the opposing team.

All this star power surrounding me was both comforting and humbling. I remember watching film with my quarterback coach, Mike White, early in my time with the Raiders. In the first series, I turned to hand off to Marcus. Then, in the next play, I passed off to Roger Craig. Finally, in the third, I tossed a swing route to Eric Dickerson.

"Holy shit, that was cool to watch," Mike commented.

"No kidding, and I had the best seat in the house," I remarked.

Several of these standouts went the extra mile to keep me in line that first year. Guys like Marcus swung by my house to roust me for practice. He was known for walking gently and carrying a big stick, and only a few people ever saw Marcus lose his temper. My childhood buddy Marco Forster was one of them, steering clear of the Super Bowl Most Valuable Player (MVP) after one memorable exchange.

It started with a phone call. I couldn't lift my head after another bender with ecstasy, cocaine, and liquor. My body felt like the Tin Man. It took all my effort to cover my face with the pillow to protect myself from the piercing sunlight. After four painful rings, Marco rolled off the bed and grabbed the phone, mostly to silence the noise.

With quarterback coach Mike White, 1991.

"Hello?" he answered, mildly confused and equally irritated. He listened for a minute, eyes dilating as he came to attention.

"Okay. This is Marco. No, Todd's not here," he explained. Another few seconds passed. "No, no, he's on his way." Another pause. "Okay, yes, will do."

Marco hung up the phone. He planted himself on the foot of the bed, where he promptly passed out in a fetal position.

"Practice?" I asked, muffled by the pillow and still unable to peel my skull from the bed. Marco didn't answer, so I conked out without a care in the world. I lay comatose for at least another twenty minutes until someone walking outside the balcony changed the balance of light in the room. I cracked one eyelid to catch Marcus's unmistakable smooth gait.

"Marco... Marco, shit," I whispered, sitting upright and tapping his ribs with my foot still stuck in the sheets.

"Wake up." I raised my voice. "Marcus Allen is coming to the fucking door." That was all it took for Marco to snap to attention. With a three-alarm fire underway, he mobilized.

His eyes darted around the room. "Oh shit, I told him you were on your way to practice." Marco went from concerned to panicked in under two seconds. He surveyed the room's corners for a hiding spot. There was nothing to camouflage his presence. He scurried into the hallway, more confused than a lost puppy, and threw himself in the front hall closet without a word. Just as the door slid shut, Marcus thumped on the front door. His force offered all the information I needed.

"Not good, Todd, not good at all," Marco whispered from his makeshift panic room as I passed en route to the front door.

"I'll handle this, don't sweat it," I said.

I opened the door to face a bug-eyed Marcus Allen who impatiently examined his watch. He looked past me, forgoing greetings in the interest of time. "Where the hell is Marco?"

I hesitated, not understanding why that mattered. "Umm, not sure," I lied, which was second nature by now.

"That little fucker must be here somewhere," Marcus said, still scanning the hallway for another carrottop, as Marco was practically a mini-me.

"No idea." I stuck with the mantra of denial.

Marcus turned his attention to his watch again. "Well, you'd better get your ass in gear. Practice starts in fifteen minutes." Marcus spun around and returned to his idling red-hot Lamborghini.

"Right behind you," I yelled as he looked back.

"Better be," he said, closing his door and hitting the gas.

After Marcus departed, Marco slid out of the closet, his orange mop in disarray. "That was close. I need a drink." He rounded the corner to the kitchen, which was peppered with half-empty Jack Daniel's bottles.

"I'm outta here," I announced, still amazed that the Super Bowl MVP had prioritized me over everything else that morning.

Two months later, Marcus didn't hold back. It was the last regular-season game of 1991 and my first series in the NFL against Kansas City. I had one of my best throws to Tim Brown for a touchdown. I trotted off the field elated but assumed this band of professionals would consider it a given. Not so. Marcus met me on the sideline, grabbing a fistful of my jersey and yanking me within earshot. "They haven't seen anything yet. You're just getting warmed up." He paused before releasing me from his grip. The sincerity and conviction in his voice could levitate the dead. It was one thing to hear of my so-called promise from commentators and hacks but quite another when it came from one of the best players in the game. Later, he compared me to Joe

Montana, suggesting I possessed the charisma required of great NFL quarterbacks. Tim Brown also weighed in, believing I had the tools for greatness.

While Marcus and Tim were in my corner, Fred Biletnikoff remained my tightest and longest-running connection with the organization. When I first locked eyes with this Raiders legend, I was a toddler, tagging along with Marv during his stint as the team's strength and conditioning coach. Fast-forward fifteen years and we chilled in the locker room, puffing away until Coach Shell shouted, "Red! Fred! Get your asses out here!"

Fred looked at me and shared with nostalgia, "Todd, you know, back in the old days when we won championships, this whole locker room lit up at halftime. And now it's just two of us." I grinned as he shook his head.

As a former wild guy in his own right, Fred wasn't overly concerned about my life outside football. But he didn't give me too much slack either. He forced me to perch on a stool during film sessions so I couldn't fall asleep. He also took me to task when I didn't deliver on the field. His rules were straightforward: he was in my corner as long as I showed up and performed.

Then there was defensive end Howie Long, who was practically an older brother. On the surface, we were polar opposites. Howie was wound like a clock, and I was a freewheeler. He was settled into family life while I was a whirling dervish. But behind the superficial, we shared an unexplainable bond.

I was swept into Howie's gravitational pull early in my first year with the Raiders, occasionally hanging out at his house on days off. The home was filled with love: there were three young boys, Chris, Kyle, and little Howie, along with his bombshell wife, Diane, who was the total package: beauty and brains.

I remember one Sunday barbecue when we settled into the living room. Howie's three boys played rough to determine the rightful owner of an action figure. Kyle took a whack at Chris to clear up the matter. While Chris was the elder son, Kyle had his dad's quick temper. Both kids would eventually land in the NFL. Howie was mid-reprimand when Diane glided in with some snacks. But I didn't notice the chips; I zeroed in on Diane cutting a swath through the living room like a runway model. She slid the bowls onto the table, smiling at the near-daily course correction. I watched her stifle a giggle. She pivoted to leave before getting pulled into the hostage release negotiations.

I instinctively wanted to take in her beauty, but Howie was one seat away. Elbows leaning on his beefy thighs, he resembled a military general about to rise from his chair. I begged my eyes not to betray me. *Look straight ahead, only at Howie. If I check out her ass, I'm a dead man.* Despite my inner dialogue, my twenty-one-year-old mind had another agenda. It was eager to engage my well-trained peripheral vision. I glanced at Howie. He looked up to smile at Diane, then my way. *Fuck, keep looking straight ahead.* As my vision veered left, I recalled a story about Howie disassembling former center Bill Lewis during practice. The guy lost his helmet, endured a brutal uppercut, and emerged from the training room with a mouthful of stitches. And that was just for talking back. If Howie caught me checking out Diane, I'd be lucky to leave their house walking.

So I did the only thing I could think of: I closed my eyes to pull the curtain on the show. By some miracle, it worked. Diane's fine frame moved out of sight, and I breathed a sigh of relief. I would make it out of Howie's alive.

While I envied his beautifully full life, nothing held me back.

By midseason, I had my road routine nailed. After the 11 PM bed check, I grabbed an ice bucket and meandered down the hall to the stairwell. If probed by the floor's security guard, I'd claim the ice maker was out of commission. Then I used the ice bucket to prop open the exit. This gave me at least twelve hours to party before the required pregame meal.

Many veterans knew I defied the rules. They usually saved me a seat to regale them with stories as the Raiders' latest court jester. Without fail, I delivered, with the tales getting wilder and raunchier as the season progressed. It was the kind of encouragement that got me into serious trouble, but they didn't know that yet.

Despite being loaded with talent, we got our asses pruned my rookie year. The 1991 season opener against the Houston Oilers at the Astrodome was eye-opening. It reminded me of a college atmosphere with over 61,000 fans chanting their fight song in a sold-out dome stadium. But that was where the similarities ended. I'd watched countless NFL games, but my position on the sideline changed everything. I knew all the players, had observed them in practice, had sweated through drills with them, and had watched them give it all. There was no weak link; every one of them was a playmaker.

I was also a fan of the competition. The Oilers had drafted my favorite college receiver, Gary Wellman. Meanwhile, the Oilers' signal-caller Warren Moon was a well-respected Los Angeles guy. An expert at delivering the ball fast, he executed movements with fluidity, wasting no time getting the ball to a five-receiver split-out. The Oilers were in the flow; they were a solid team. Meanwhile, we never found our footing that day. Quarterback Jay Schroeder threw several interceptions and spent much of the game on the sidelines while Vince Evans finished the job. All told, it was a humiliating 47–17 defeat. Even the commentator suggested the film would be burned back in Los Angeles.

In college, this type of ass-whipping made for a hellish journey home. Not with these professionals. There was no pointing fingers, sulking, or whining. It was time to learn and move on. Film reviews and lessons would come soon enough. So we kicked back on the trip home, parking football talk.

The most amusing part of those plane rides was the runway fashion show upon boarding. You'd think there was an award for the most colorfully dressed. The wide receivers weren't exactly understated, while the defensive backs went all out. Free safety Eddie Anderson and his crew sauntered on in oversized fur coats, weighed down with jewelry. They finished the look with rhinestone-encrusted shoes or tricked-out kicks. In contrast, the trench workers often wore lumberjack shirts, jeans, and boots. With a mentality that matched their positions, they were all practicality, no flash.

As a rookie, I inevitably found myself near two people movers toward the back of the plane. Once airborne, I moved around, playing card games and listening to animated stories. Linebacker Jerry Robinson, a true entertainer with the most exaggerated gestures, told the best gut-busting tales. He could make anything funny. Other guys set up players' lounges in the tight space with tables popping up like weeds. They dropped two seats flat and laid out blankets to establish the makeshift lounge. Once the seat belt sign went off, the games began. Eddie and his posse ran the high-dollar tables while offensive guard Max Montoya and his gang kept it to dollar bets. And, of course, the drinks flowed in concert with the ribbing and laughter. Defensive end Greg Townsend was known for his Grand Marnier, while the linemen shared Jack Daniel's, Crown Royal, and Absolut. I couldn't park my love for Jack but never took it too far in this crowd.

Even with the revelry, the signs of carnage couldn't be ignored. It wasn't uncommon to see trainers Todd Sperber and Rod Martin hovering around a reclined seat. They fixed quick patch jobs from the game while Dr. Robert Rosenfeld administered the 'caine brothers—Xylocaine, lidocaine, and novocaine.

The maimed were a subtle reminder of what could happen on any given day. I remember veteran offensive tackle Steve Wright weaving down the aisle with a violet welt for a mouth. The generally affable oversized human had crisscross stitches throughout his piehole. He'd started a fight with the Chief's Bill Maas that had turned into a bench-clearing brawl. Guys gave him ample room as makeshift medics went to work. Nearly every player looked away, knowing it could've been them and might be someday.

Then there were the genuinely horrifying injuries that were even more difficult to forget. The year before I joined the franchise, I saw Bo Jackson suffer a brutal career-ending hip injury. It happened during a playoff game against the Cincinnati Bengals. A rogue tackle ended his thirty-four-yard run with a force strong enough to dislocate his hip. If it were any other running back, he would have gone down, but not Bo. He fought through it, pulling it further out of joint as he struggled for freedom and more yards. And since Bo could do almost anything, he popped it back into place after the whistle. He instantly left every fan and player forever wondering what could've been.

Injuries of every degree were far too common. They were so frequent that when a man went down in practice, we just advanced the line. It was heartless and insensitive. It felt akin to leaving dead bodies on the battlefield. And I never shook the sound of grown men screaming in agony. Inevitably, they were stuck on the bottom of a pyramid of linemen, twisted into impossible shapes. Then I heard the injured teammate howling in the training room, doctors pulling parts in every direction.

There were also bruised egos that emerged from the locker room after the occasional attitude adjustment. Think of it as a chiropractic visit for excessive confidence. It often started with a teammate's strutting, shit-talking, and bad-mouthing. These were the universal signals that a guy needed to be leveled to rejoin the mere mortals. It didn't matter if players were rookies or veterans; no one was immune to the famed adjustment. Once an offender was diagnosed, several teammates cornered the player and drove him into his locker for a loving pounding—nothing on the face, just some body shots to realign his thinking. After watching these occur a time or two, I decided to keep any feelings about my abilities to myself.

I was also careful to respect the defensive DJ in the sanctum, as Greg Townsend controlled the tunes. Greg was cool, street cool—the original *Straight Outta Compton*. He was the kind of guy who got what he wanted—someone I didn't mess with because if you crossed him, you'd hear about it quickly. On very rare occasions, he gave me the green light to play a song or two, but otherwise he controlled the soul and funk, which was a far cry from my usual grunge. So, more often than not, I listened to my Walkman, jamming to the beat, usually Nirvana or Mudhoney.

I steered clear of the interior offensive and defensive linemen during the pregame period. Most of those animals went to dark places to get cranked. They pounded coffees, beat their chests, and talked loads of shit. In contrast, the quarterbacks, receivers, and defensive backs stayed relaxed and loose. They kept the conversations light, with free-flowing jokes and a calm aura. There was no need to waste energy getting the amperage up too soon. It wasn't until we got to the tunnel that everyone ratcheted up the intensity, sweating in anticipation of our version of gladiator games.

As much as I loved being part of a team, I was fined heartily for rebellious acts, including cutting my sleeves, leaving my shirt out, and pulling down my socks. Wild, right? Forget about individualism in the NFL. They ran a tight ship. Conformity was part of the arrangement. I was also fined for tossing balls into the crowd: $1,500 for the first offense and then $3,000 the next time. I pressed on despite the punishments and mounting expenses.

In week sixteen, while everyone else minded curfew, I joined four airline stewardesses on Bourbon Street, downing hurricanes and rolling on ecstasy. By game time against the Saints, I was desperately hungover and barely functioning. Warm-ups were a trudge through quicksand. I couldn't remember play details if my life depended on it. But there was nothing to worry about, or so I thought. Jay Schroeder's backup was Vince Evans, a former Trojan. He was a veteran drafted by the Chicago Bears when I was a shy seven-year-old. I brought up the rear as the third-stringer and the baby of the bunch. So I bet against myself ever getting the nod my first season . . . until Jay injured his ankle.

During the calamity, Coach Shell shot me an eager look. The "Are you ready?" face. *Oh shit.* They wanted me in. This was an important game; we were in the running for a playoff spot. I panicked and waved him off. If I went in, they'd see I didn't have the playbook committed to memory. Remarkably, they never probed about my reluctance to enter the shit show—an epic beatdown at 27–0. I dodged a bullet.

Eventually, I was ready when we took on the Kansas City Chiefs, who had an identical 9–6 record. While they'd beaten us earlier in the season, the right to host a playoff game was up for grabs. Everyone wanted to win, but it was do-or-die for me; my off-field friendship with Flea of the Red Hot Chili Peppers meant I'd be backstage when Nirvana opened their concert in Los Angeles the following weekend. If we lost, I'd be in a hotel room in Kansas City while my dream bands took the stage. It would be almost unimaginable to miss the concert.

Luckily, the deciding game was on our turf in the Coliseum, my second home. As soon as Coach announced midweek that I would start the game, my answering machine blew up. Former teammates, buddies, acquaintances, and even friends I didn't know I had hit me up for tickets. They didn't realize that I only got four freebies per game. I went all out, buying at least thirty. I didn't want to leave anyone hanging for my debut in the big time.

As excited as I was, I couldn't deny one nagging problem: I wasn't an optimal fit for the Raiders' style of play. I knew it, and plenty of other guys did too. Riki Ellison, Roger Craig, and Ronnie Lott, all previously part of the San Francisco 49ers dynasty, acknowledged my predicament. They came from a team where the quarterback got the ball to the athletes fast: throw two and run for eighty. In contrast, the Raiders often went for a play-action fake, followed by a seven-step drop-back and a deep throw to the fastest guys. The mantra "speed kills" was the Raiders' way. This worked great in the sixties and seventies, but defenses had evolved. Holding the ball that long was a dangerous proposition.

Initiation time.

How could I be successful in this environment? Tim Brown. He was the critical piece to my puzzle. No matter what, I needed Tim on the field. He was tough and talented. No one worked harder for the ball. So I fell back on my Mater Dei ways and went for my open guy, especially during my first start against the Chiefs.

Sure, I had some nerves before game time, but nothing insurmountable as I took the field for the Raiders' first offensive series. One of the Chiefs' guys, Neil Smith, with legs thicker than tree trunks, celebrated my start with copious shit-talking. He lit into me and didn't shut up.

"I'm going to make quick work of you, pretty boy," he announced, glaring at me as he launched into his verbal carving. He was amped and ready for action, frothing at the mouth and rolling his neck with crazy eyes similar to Marv's after the Huntington Beach incident.

I couldn't resist a retort. "Sure you are, Neil. Keep talking, and I'll wear your old ass out."

If he didn't put out a hit on me before that comment, he sure as hell did after that jab. I'd committed the cardinal sin, which Marv explained after the game: never, ever verbally engage with defensive linemen. It escalates the situation from professional to personal in a heartbeat. And so, I dug a hole and kept at it all game, firing up Neil's furnace with every word.

With the Raiders behind 7–0 in the first quarter, I completed a drive followed by a twenty-six-yard touchdown pass to my guy, Tim. He made the throw appear flawless, finding the perfect spot. As for me, I had a reputation for openly celebrating my best throws like a little kid—jumping into any available arms and pumping my fist—and this one was no exception. Along with joy, I felt a wave of relief to have this first one under my belt. The momentum shifted in our favor as I eyed a large sign in the crowd reading "Todd 'the Snake' Marinovich." Then the Chiefs rifled off thirteen unanswered points to put us at 20–7. Eventually, Neil gave me a painful welcome to the NFL, exacting revenge when he pile-drove me to the ground. It felt like I'd been hit by a runaway logging truck. My body folded, and my head bounced off the grass—lights out. Even the color commentator called out the exceptional blindside. For the first few seconds, I couldn't see a thing. Then I heard Marcus and felt him lift me to my knees.

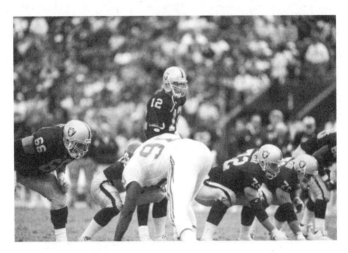

The Chiefs' Neil Smith (number ninety) on the hunt.

"Just make it back to the huddle. I got this," he whispered in my earhole.

With his help, I headed toward the blob of bodies. I fought to regain my vision and composure. Jerseys and faces were fuzzy, but I heard Marcus call the play and break the huddle. Then he leaned in and whispered, "Toss the ball off to me. We're good."

I nodded and found my way behind our country-strong center, Don Mosebar. By this point, I could make out faces, but they were all expressionless as my mind worked to catch up. I wouldn't let my team down, especially not Marcus, who refused to let me falter. I executed the play without a hitch, running a flat little swing route as my mental fog began to clear. Reenergized after this advance, I went for it on the next of the series, launching a spiral to Ethan Horton in the end zone for a touchdown. And then later another to Tim. While it was a painful loss at 27–21, I delivered a formidable performance and displayed a fair bit of resilience. I completed 23 of 40 passes for 243 yards with 3 touchdowns without a single interception. The loss was bad, but the worst part was giving up my concert tickets to Marco while I'd be jacking off in a hotel room in Kansas City.

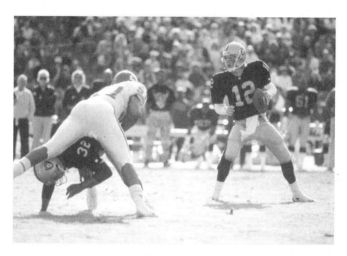

Marcus Allen buying me time.

Then came the wild-card game played in the groan-worthy Arrowhead Stadium where I became the first Raider rookie to start a playoff game on December 28, 1991. It was a cold and hostile environment made worse by the surface. It was like playing on a painted basketball court that allowed the outside linebacker Derrick Thomas to move with inhuman ability.

The Chiefs benefited from a week to adjust based on my obvious desire to get Tim the ball. They wisely positioned a robber—a safety playing at linebacker—who foiled my plans. It cost us three interceptions since Tim and I couldn't always find the same holes.

After nearly three hours of trench warfare, there was one final drive for the chance to win it. Given my many intercepted throws, any reasonable person would suspect I'd crumble under pressure. But people didn't realize that the same thing that made me an addict helped me on the turf. I easily let go of, heck, even completely forgot, my mistakes, as if I had borderline amnesia. Any humiliation or shame was vapor as I returned to the well without fear. But the universe wasn't in our favor yet again, as we fell short after a flag bonanza: holding, illegal motion, more holding, and on it went. We didn't have to rely on the Chiefs to beat us; we accomplished that on our own. This marked the third loss to our biggest rivals in a year.

A rough day in Kansas City.

This wasn't how I wanted to end the 1991 season, but I had other things on my mind.

Off the field, I lived an entirely different existence. I partied with rock stars, slept with Playboy Bunnies, and experienced unfettered access to nearly anything in Los Angeles. Through my connections at record labels, I frequented concerts, rubbing shoulders with colorful characters backstage, from actors to artists and other celebrities. I usually ended my nights at the always popular Chateau Marmont or, better yet, the Viper Room. That's where Gary Oldman introduced me to Charlie Sheen. I became a regular at Charlie's Malibu house. It was the perfect bachelor pad, with batting cages in the backyard, a full arcade, a billiard room, and even a shooting range in the basement. It was a pretty sweet existence; we spent most of our time playing games in between lines of coke and leggy models.

The connection was so solid that Charlie eventually offered me his limo driver. "Whatever you do, don't drive fucked up. Use my guy," he said, handing me the driver's card after another bender at the Viper Room.

"Thanks," I responded with appreciation. I saved those digits and dialed them often. The poor driver crisscrossed the city most nights with Charlie, me, and other celebrities in the mix. His ride service was one of the only reasons that aspect of my record remained relatively clean.

Outside of the drugs, Charlie was a great influence. He surrounded himself with good dudes who appreciated a nice meal before the debauchery. Spending so much time in his wake, I had plenty of opportunities to watch him handle uncomfortable situations, which usually involved paparazzi or hecklers. He was so smooth and unbothered. It blew me away how well he handled fame after decades in the spotlight. But there was one notable exception. We were at dinner and Charlie seemed a bit out of sorts—he was fidgety and his eyes darted around the restaurant. A guy approached our table and launched into Charlie. "You can't act for shit. The only reason you're even on the screen is because of your fricking dad."

He'd heard it all before, but his reaction was different this time. Charlie twitched, turned his chair toward the antagonist, and blew his top like a well-shaken Coke bottle, releasing decades of pent-up rage. "Who do you think you are?" Charlie snarled. His throbbing eyes zeroed in, with the calculation of a tiger ready to lunge. As he rose, two of our dinner guests restrained Charlie. The guy backed off fast, but the damage was done. It took several hours of partying, lines, and hookers to get Charlie back down to his set point.

I also had my fair share of hecklers. They only seemed to emerge at awkward times, like the night I brought a date to a Kings game. I was really into this chick, so I wanted her to be impressed by a memorable date. After dinner at the Forum Club, we shimmied along the glass to our seats. Everything went to plan until a guy several rows up shouted, "Hey, Marinovich, I heard you got more snow than Baldy this year." I looked down and kept moving, but my date heard it all. She barely made eye contact the rest of the night. Not surprisingly, she never answered my calls for another rendezvous.

While this girl wanted nothing to do with me, my Raiders credentials usually served as keys to the City of Angels. They got me through velvet ropes, backstage, and into dressing rooms for some of my favorite acts. I was always excited, but never as much as at one Neil Young concert at the Hollywood Bowl. His music spoke to my heart and carried me through many long nights. I even drew Neil's portrait, reimagining a young photo of him, shaggy haired with penetrating eyes. While fine-tuning my work, I decided it belonged in Neil's hands.

My opportunity arrived during my second year with the Raiders. I joined a few high school and college buddies for a wild doubleheader night in the Hollywood Hills. It started with a pit stop at USC to secure some acid.

"I think this stuff's weak, so you might want to take two," my source warned, sliding a small paper envelope into my hands outside the trusty Five-O.

Marco nodded as Dirty Curty flashed me a thumbs-up. Curty was a college teammate. Fast as lightning on the turf, he possessed a chill surf cowboy vibe off the field.

"If you say so." I discreetly dropped a double dose onto my tongue.

I walked back to Curty's beat-up old Caddy, not giving the exchange another thought as I shared the instructions and goods with the rest of my crew. It was an entertaining ride to the Bowl, with nearly everyone hallucinating as the hills shape-shifted and palm trees came alive. By the time we parked and entered the Bowl, the night sky was talking back. This wouldn't be a big deal at one of Neil's typical concerts, but it was just him, a guitar, and a piano this time. While the crowd was suitably mellow, my crew was anything but appropriate and was frying balls.

Backstage after the concert, I was ready to meet Neil. Marco, however, didn't even know his own name. If I was out in left field, he wasn't even in the stadium. He was too cooked to move or speak, so I left him with Flea while I found another co-conspirator. I wouldn't miss a chance that might never come again. I looked over to Curty, and he nodded, ready to mobilize. We trailed security as they cleared the way. I wasn't nervous until we encountered the dressing room door. I'd be face-to-face with the legend once it opened. I couldn't bring myself to knock, so Curty did the honors, delivering a surprisingly gentle rap as he keyed into my growing trepidation.

The door cracked open a few inches and a graying man peered out, ready to run interference. He looked like a hobbit peeking out of its hole. Still tripping hard, I watched this bug-eyed creature's lips move, spewing gibberish.

"Who are you guys?" he pressed, looking at Curty and then my way. His beady eyes betrayed him, flickering with irritation at two raggedy punks eager for entry.

"Todd Marinovich to see Neil," Curty sounded off. I swallowed past the horse-pill-sized lump in my throat as the sentinel ran another visual scan.

He shrugged, suggesting that he'd never heard of me.

The door closed for a few seconds as we overheard faint murmuring. Then it reopened and the same haggard face, tougher than beef jerky, cracked a smile. "Come on in, boys." He stepped aside, revealing something akin to an opium den with a sizable earth-toned rug and a kitchenette tucked into one corner. Neil hovered over a small pot, making tea.

Meanwhile, two bombshell blondes sat perched on the edge of the couch, listening attentively to the master. Curty didn't hesitate, nestling between the beauties like a dog who'd found his rightful home. I took a different tack, respectfully sitting cross-legged on the rug as if preparing for another kind of trip. I sheepishly extended the tube to Neil while my eyes darted around the strange space.

"I have something for you," I opened with deference.

"Thanks," he responded, placing the tube on the counter. He

had no intention of opening the gift, as the hotties on the couch still needed their tea.

"Aren't you going to see what it is?" one of the babes probed.

I wasn't sure if I wanted to be there to witness his reaction. I was proud, but I was still refining my artistic instincts. It would be a blow to my ego if he shrugged it off.

"Yeah, sure," he responded, still far more interested in the chicks.

He finished brewing the tea and then unrolled my pencil drawing. His thick eyebrows peaked with pleasure while his muttonchops spread, making room for his growing smile. In my altered state, Neil's facial hair looked like worms noodling around on his weathered face. I wanted to look away, but I was transfixed.

I have no idea how long I sat there staring at his annelid-ridden face. The drugs elongated and retracted time, bending it beyond comprehension. Finally, the sound of Neil's voice interrupted my trip.

"This is great, kid. I love it." Then he paused and pivoted: "After tea, let's head to Pink's."

I never understood why celebrities loved this hot dog joint on Sunset, but they flocked in hordes for meat that made Marv cringe. I respectfully declined, and Curty—still cooked—took the hint. With my mission accomplished, we'd join Flea at his place in the Hollywood Hills.

Five of us returned to Curty's ride and tailed Flea's Mercedes sedan plastered with punk rock bumper stickers. In all my years up to that point and since, I have never encountered a tricked-out Mercedes with hard-core rock bumper stickers. That was Flea: brilliant, complex, and never one to fit neatly into societal norms.

As we careened down the streets in our beat-up old land

yacht, I slid around the back seat, watching the world spin. I noticed Curty doing the same with one minor difference: he was driving, hands barely on the wheel. Meanwhile, his eyes were everywhere but on the road. I shouted for him to hit the brake as he barreled toward Flea, who'd stopped at a red light. Confused, Curty accelerated before promptly pasting the brake to the floor mat. The beast of a vehicle had the response time of a battleship. We slid, fully perpendicular, toward Flea's beautifully decorated ass end. *Oh fuck.*

Moving with the grace of a hippo, I braced for impact. The Caddy angrily resisted the sudden braking, finally coming to a full stop only inches from Flea's ride. It was divine intervention; the universe wouldn't ruin this epic night.

We howled with fear mixed with laughter as we brushed off this near miss. With the gods in our favor, we made it to Flea's house without a scratch. His place was a 1930s Los Angeles ranch-style home, understated for a platinum-album-winning star. And the interior was even more stark, with a bare minimum of furniture. The only thing on the wall was a massive painting by guitarist John Frusciante, a former bandmate whose drug addiction had pulled him away from the group. Even though they'd separated professionally, Flea paid homage to the future great, who eventually reunited with the band.

As the night rolled on, my mind cleared. I noticed a pile of gold records in frames stacked along the wall. Not a single one hung in any self-worship space. There was just one tacky award on his fireplace mantel: MTV's Rock N' Jock B-Ball Jam MVP. I knew he loved hoops, but seriously?

Aside from having a few drinks, Flea was remarkably sober, politely declining our acid because he had a court case the next day in Miami. It wasn't for him; his bandmate Anthony Kiedis had exposed himself during a recent show. He would testify and support his longtime brother from another mother.

While Flea didn't partake, I decided his place was the ideal setting for some kind herb, so I ventured into the backyard to take a pull off a glass bong. On cloud nine, I joined a game of ping-pong, where the remnants of my acid trip flared. The ball turned into a solid white stripe that took an eternity to hit my paddle. And when it did, it sounded like a drum. Even when the ball was nowhere near me, I heard the call of a kick drum. It was turning into a wild trip, so I dropped the paddle and followed a sound reminiscent of a call to battle.

I ventured through the house, up a ladder, and finally through a trapdoor to discover a hidden music studio. I stood dumbfounded, watching Flea on a bass guitar and Marco on drums decorated with the Raiders' silver-and-black shield. They took turns soloing, producing a friendly musical banter. Once they wrapped, I nodded with deep admiration. "I'd kill for a recording of that," I said.

Flea grinned and explained, "The best music is never captured." Coming from this grand master, the words stirred me to smile and honor his greatness with a respectful bow.

From that night forward, I found my place in Flea's world. He taught me to play the bass, and we would take walks to the local outdoor proving ground to join late-night pickup games. We spent hours, deep into the double digits, on those courts tearing it up. We were both great shots from the outside, leaving our defenders shaking their heads. During one of the craziest times in my journey, this was one of a handful of friendships that didn't revolve around drugs. For that, I was forever thankful.

While my world felt chaotic, the city around me also experienced plenty of mayhem. The beating of Rodney King rightfully rocked Los Angeles. Once ashes from the city riots sprinkled down on my Manhattan Beach pad, I turned on the news to watch the coverage. I'd never expected things to get personal. I approached the screen, rubbing my eyes in disbelief.

"What the heck?" I asked no one in particular. A few of my college buddies kicked back on the couch, and Matt Gee leaned in, focusing on the TV.

"That's one fubar situation," Matt said.

The news replayed some of the horrors captured in the aftermath, including a guy pulled from his semitruck and savagely beaten at the intersection of Florence and Normandie. I craned my neck to decipher a familiar face.

There, in the middle of the action, was the bouncer from the Five-O. "No way. That's Vance," I announced, eyeing his large frame and distinctive gait.

"It can't be," Matt Gee insisted, pitching forward and squinting at the screen.

"It's definitely him." I circled the guy with my finger like a coach calling out a delinquent player.

Vance was anything but a racist. We partied together plenty at the Five-O, and the difference in our skin color was never an issue. He would've been a teammate with his build and strength in a different time and place. Instead, he got to punch his card in prison.

Lucky for me, I wasn't raised to judge people on anything but their skills. This started with Marv during his training and scouting of star players. Plenty of powerhouses joined our dinner table during those early years, but one stood out among the rest: my future head coach, Art Shell.

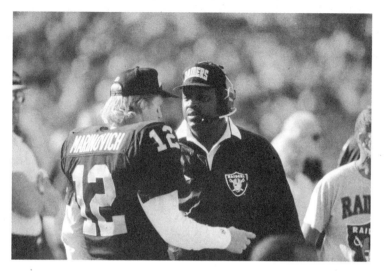

Getting on the same page with Coach Shell.

He joined the Raiders as a third-round draft pick and completed a strong fourteen-year playing career. Then he worked his way up the ranks, becoming one of the first African American NFL head coaches in the modern era. This was one of many examples of values that set the Raiders apart from other franchises. The original owner was a self-made man driven to bring football to the working town of Oakland. The Señors—whose name was later changed to the Raiders—played on a pock-ridden and often muddy field, making barely enough to survive. The naysayers lined up to challenge the team's viability, but the guys on the field, along with the coach and men in the front office, wouldn't give up. It was more than a business; it was a mission.

Fast-forward a few decades, and the team found its missing link in Al Davis. He was a live-or-die football fanatic and a renegade in his own right. With the mystique of a mob boss, he played the part well, slicking back his hair and donning expensive sunglasses and heavy cologne. He drove around Oakland in a black

Caddy with tinted windows and no license plates. As a street-smart guy from Brooklyn, he didn't give a fuck about anything except football. He also had an outsized chip on his shoulder that drove him to prove everyone wrong. His "us versus them" outlier mentality flowed from his pores, first as head coach and then as managing general partner. Eventually, he called all the shots as the franchise's majority owner. He didn't just want to win; he intended to dominate, and in many regards, he succeeded.

The fans shared Al's passion for the Raiders. I learned this lesson repeatedly during walks through the Coliseum parking lot. I was accustomed to the Saturday crowds. They were straight out of a country-club brochure, with well-coifed hair, flawless complexions, finely appointed sweater sets, and Oxford loafers. Their chatter while tailgating in the lots ranged from investment strategies to ski chalets and second homes.

In contrast, Sundays were more akin to a stroll through San Quentin State Prison's level-four yard. The misfits, renegades, and nonconformists flocked to the Coliseum with unmatched enthusiasm. Everyone from accountants to dockworkers transformed into Mad Max characters with spiked leather gear and elaborately painted faces. More about the pageantry than the eats, they dipped burned hot dogs in beers and sopped it up with bad potato chips. And forget finances—they talked plain-language shit and plenty of it. These were my people, with a few exceptions.

I met my first aberrations when leaving the tunnel at the tail end of the 1991 season. As I navigated the fans requesting autographs, I tried to keep moving. After a few slow-paced signings, four rough-looking guys blocked my path, stopping me dead in my tracks. Their reputations must have preceded them, as the rest of the crowd obediently stepped back. In my estimation, one of two things was about to happen: a mugging at knifepoint or an embrace tighter than from a long-lost brother.

I was wide of the mark on both counts. I eyed each of them, hoping to identify the ringleader. A heavily tattooed, apparent alpha stepped forward. I rapidly scanned the incoming threat: he looked like a young Suge Knight with an outlined teardrop tattoo below his eye—the gang symbol for an attempted murder. *Great.* My best option was to appear relaxed, a near-impossible feat. I did my best and offered a nod of respect, aka a "please don't kill me" greeting.

I waited for him to speak first. He leaned in so close that I smelled the sour tequila on his breath and noticed the edges of a crescent-shaped scar peeking out from his shirt. "You just say the word, and we'll take care of it."

"It?" I wondered aloud. I took in every detail of his face, searching for more clues.

"Schroeder." He paused and looked around before continuing. "You give the signal, and we'll take out Jay Schroeder."

"What?" I stepped back. It took me a second to process this proposal. If it were anyone else, I'd laugh, but they were dead fucking serious.

His eyes, inhumanly dark, were eager for a response. I had to be clear with my message.

"Nah, man, it's good. I'll earn that starting spot, don't you worry." I paused and leaned closer to reiterate my message: "No need to do anything." I wanted to emphasize this point to protect Jay. These fans' commitment to excellence was at the next level, far exceeding Al's high bar.

The guy nodded reluctantly. I finally let down my guard and smiled. "It's all good, man. Hang in there." He wasn't the jovial type, but I had to lighten the mood. As much as I needed to defend Jay, I knew firsthand how feelings about quarterbacks changed. Jay might be on the chopping block now, but I could easily be next.

"Okay." He backed up and signaled to his crew. With that, they bled into the crowd, vanishing as quickly as they'd appeared.

I bet anything those diehards were still itching to off Jay at the start of the rocky 1992 season. Frustrations in the locker room mounted when Howie finally shared the front office's decision. "Jay, you're done. We're going with the kid." Crickets. You could hear a pin drop. My eyes rested on Jay. I felt terrible about this public rebuke. He took it well, though. He offered a quick acknowledgment and grimace, as if taking a pull of NyQuil. He'd probably heard it from Coach Shell beforehand, but this verbal punch in front of the team had to hurt.

As swiftly as teammates looked at Jay, their gazes came my way. Most smiled, but there were equal measures of confidence and questions. I was a gamble: an immature, barely legal hopeful. Several guys in that locker room had kids older than me. Guard Max Montoya, for one, was quick to remind me in the huddle. Other guys were losing their hair or turning gray, while I possessed the unpredictable mane of youth.

Too young or too soon, I had to answer the doubters. So, on September 20, 1992, at the tender age of twenty-three, I became the Raiders' youngest quarterback of the era to start an NFL game. I was up against the Browns, then coached by Bill Belichick and a little-known defensive coordinator named Nick Saban. The Browns threw their entire playbook our way during what turned into a demolition derby.

Their running back Eric Metcalf managed an impressive four touchdowns. And their prized linebacker Clay Matthews, a former Trojan, turned into a highly paid hitman with me in his crosshairs.

Our offensive moments of greatness were few and far between, but I threw my first touchdown of the year to the speedster wideout Willie Gault. I also set a Raiders record of thirty-three completions (it was later broken but still a solid showing). Yet it wasn't enough to get us out of a deep hole. We came up empty in another battle, losing 27–16.

A narrow escape.

The nagging talons of the NFL's substance abuse program compounded my growing on-field frustrations. It rested on a four-legged policy involving deterrence, medical screening, education, and treatment. Sounds comprehensive, but who were they kidding? In practice, it was all about testing. A positive result sent a player into the program, along with support services, aka rehab, in the offseason. But in my case, I was a presumed positive from the start. I lived under the league's thumb my entire tenure, donating urine five days a week under the watchful eye of a retired police officer. While my treatment was grossly unfair, I suspect my cocaine arrest before the draft was to blame. Another theory, rarely discussed, had to do with payback. Putting me in the program before a violation was the league's way of sticking it to Al Davis, their insider antagonist. While they couldn't punish him directly, as Al's boy, I was fair game.

Wising up fast, I turned to lysergic acid diethylamide (LSD) most weekends since it was undetectable. I also devised a near-foolproof scheme to avoid a positive result for other substances. My close friends helped me out with their urine samples, which lined my refrigerator. Then I emptied these deposits into travel-sized sunscreen bottles with squirt tops. Since cold pee raised flags, I'd drop the bottle into a warm cup of coffee at the Raiders facility. After shooting the shit with the guys, Mr. Wizz-ard, the pee collector, would inevitably appear for my deposit. Keeping the sunscreen bottle hidden below my junk, I'd ask him to turn on the sink faucet and I'd talk football to keep him distracted. It worked like magic. Any time he turned around, he saw the flow coming from my groin. Since no guy wanted to inspect another's junk thoroughly, I was good to go. That was, of course, until a few tests didn't go quite as planned.

Things went sideways during the lead-up to the September 28, 1992, game against the Chiefs at Arrowhead Stadium. I opened my refrigerator on Friday morning to a bone-dry wasteland, having carelessly used up all the clean urine. I had to find someone to cover me, as I was far from clean. I rounded the corner to the living room to discover Matt Gee out cold on the couch. He'd drunk the night before, but at least there wouldn't be any drugs resulting in an automatic failure. So I rousted Matt, who was heavier than a pile of dumbbells. Of course, he obliged, and I headed to the facility with some fresh goods.

After depositing the piss for analysis, I went about my business, not giving it another thought until Sunday, when I arrived at the Raiders facility. I headed to the locker room to prepare for the morning walk-through before the game flight. But as my foot hit the grass, two junior assistants in stiff Raiders polos barreled toward me with looks of utter disbelief.

"Todd, you have to come with us," the taller one ordered as he guided me to a waiting car.

"What's up, guys?" I asked, quickly surmising that this must be related to my 7 AM deposit two days prior, which had been sent to the Olympic training center for analysis.

"You were four times over the legal limit. The protocol is to take you to the hospital."

Matt fucking Gee, damn it. That beast could drink more than anyone else I knew. I should've considered this possible outcome. It would not end well. I was in a catch-22. If I denied intoxication, I'd have to explain that the piss wasn't mine. On the other hand, if I went along with the charade, they might send me to treatment. I'd do just about anything to avoid it.

So I fell back on my go-to mantra: deny, deny, deny. "No way, it had to be an error," I explained. It was useless. They followed orders from on high, as in NFL headquarters. The driver made fast tracks to Centinela Hospital in Inglewood, California. He entered the semicircle, stopping shy of the waiting attendants. Buckle up for detox, the worst kind of dopamine fast.

Thirty minutes later, I lay flat in a sterile room, with doctors and their soft dog eyes debating a path forward while my team boarded a flight to Kansas City. I spent the next sixteen hours in the hospital with plenty of time to run through the gamut of emotions. Frustration, irritation, anxiety, you name it—I felt them all before finally dozing off around midnight.

The next morning, I woke drenched in sweat. I was late to practice, a recurring nightmare. Except this time, it was true. Not only had I skipped practice, I was also about to miss an important game against our rivals.

I'd lost hope by 5 AM, but that's precisely when fate stepped in. The doctors, now fully aware of my sobriety, granted me safe passage and contacted the Raiders. Thirty minutes later, the same driver picked me up at the discharge station. But this time, he ushered me to the airport for a private flight to Kansas City.

I have no idea how I kept my shit together on that flight. My nerves dipped in parabolic arcs. I couldn't sit still as I debated how Al Davis might manage the situation. *Would he fire me on the spot? Bench me indefinitely? Laugh it off?* All responses were possible, but I never expected what came to pass: that I would kick off as quarterback.

I was wholly unprepared for my fifteenth start since high school, at a time when I should've still been in college. My world was upside down as I fought to compartmentalize the hospital drama. I had to focus on leading the team—a near-impossible task given the pregame ordeal. Everyone, including me, wanted to paper over my addiction. So I stuffed my emotions deep within the well and delivered a mixed performance, as did the rest of the Raiders. Eric Dickerson ran the ball into the end zone for an early but brief lead before the Chiefs knocked the snot out of us with a painful final score of 27–7.

Not long after came the 1990 NFL champion New York Giants. This game had special meaning because of an inside joke shared with Marv. Any time I struggled with other teams during my youth, he always said, "It's not like you're playing the New York Giants." Well, this time, I was. I had to call.

"Guess who I'm playing today, Marv?" I said, forgoing a greeting.

He laughed. "Yeah, yeah, the New York Giants." I heard him puttering in the kitchen, making something more medicinal than tasty. I could re-create the scene from memory, I'd witnessed it so many times.

"And guess who I'm going to beat?" I added.

"Attaboy. My guess would be the New York Giants. Now get to work," he said, still chuckling.

My record as a starter was less than favorable at 0–4, so the skeptics chomped at the bit as we entered the matchup. The first half of the game fell to New York and my haters. But Marcus delivered a fiery speech at halftime to motivate the team. It worked, and we secured two field goals and a short out to Tim for a sixty-eight-yard touchdown in the fourth quarter. We eked out a 13–10 win without a single interception.

My mission was accomplished in more ways than one. I joined my family at a local USC watering hole after the game to celebrate the win. Without warning, Marv leaned in with an earnest expression consuming his face. I sensed something important was about to go down.

"I am so proud of you." Marv paused, registering the surprise on my face, and then continued. "You have exceeded every expectation I ever had for you."

His words hit so deep that I wobbled on my stool and blinked back decades of emotion that rose to the surface. I honestly never thought this moment would come. I savored his words as they softened every bit of childhood trauma lodged in my cells.

Nothing else needed to be said. We both fell silent for several seconds as drinkers at other tables produced meaningless noise, unconcerned with the profound implications of our shared moment. It signaled a tectonic shift in my life. Like Marv, I felt my mission was complete. I'd accomplished everything I wanted in football: to play at the highest level and, more importantly, to receive Marv's full-throated approval, which I'd chased for over two decades. As we left the bar that evening, everything felt different, yet the season was far from over.

Despite my waning interest in football, the next week I completed eleven of twenty-one passes with two touchdowns to Eric Dickerson and Tim Brown against the Buffalo Bills for a 20–3 win.

Then I was injured during a road game against the Seahawks. Their fans proved to be some of the most lethal in the league. Chants echoed throughout the cement chamber, making it nearly impossible to change plays. I realized this a moment too late when I called an audible on the line. Center Don Mosebar didn't hear the adjustment over the crowd, even though I was so close with both hands up in his crotch. I pulled away at one, and Don held the ball just long enough for the noseguard Cortez Kennedy to blow by and crush me. My leg planted, refusing to move, but my knee had other plans. The most upsetting part was knowing that my careless call had caused the injury.

Musical chairs started again, with Jay sliding into position and generating an impressive 19–0 victory. This win gave us some light in the tunnel, with a 3–4 record and the remote possibility of a third consecutive playoff season. The future Super Bowl champion Dallas Cowboys had other plans, though.

Throwing heat to Tim Brown.

Then came my final NFL start and a painful game in all regards on November 8, 1992. We matched up against the Eagles, who loved to prey on young quarterbacks. With the second-worst turnover ratio in the league, they were ready to feast on the Raiders.

My first interception was a bounce off Willie Gault's hands as if they weren't attached. It wasn't necessarily my fault, but so it goes. After that, I was practically bird-dogging Tim. And then came the second and third interceptions; well, they weren't pretty, as our offense collapsed. After my third interception, the coaching staff had seen enough risky football. They pulled me from the game, with Jay securing the starting position for the remainder of the season.

While the 1991 and 1992 seasons didn't end well, I fared far worse. I landed in rehab during both offseasons after failed urine tests.

The first time, it caught me off guard. Naive as hell, I took the message at face value: I was instructed to show up in Orange County for media interviews. Easy enough—I might even drop by Mom's for dinner after I finished with the reporters. I entered the hotel thinking about food and headed toward the assigned suite. Nothing seemed unusual until I opened the door to face Mom, Marv, Marcus, Howie, and my agent, Mike Barnett, staring back at me in an evenly spaced semicircle. It looked worse than a low-budget funeral.

What the fuck? Forget about hunger; my fight-or-flight instinct spiked. I could feel my skin heat up—this would not be good.

"Hey, all," I announced, clinging to the doorknob and refusing to let go of the only exit out of this trap.

"Come in and take a seat," Mike invited me with eager eyes. Meanwhile, Marv's eyebrows twitched, indicating his growing frustration.

"I'm good standing right here," I stated, entering the space and planting myself outside the circle, unwilling to sit in the one open chair opposing this inquisition. "I'm good," I reiterated as if stating it for the record.

"Things are far from good, Todd," Mike responded, setting the tone. It was code for "buckle up." There was no mistaking the concern in his eyes as he fidgeted in his chair.

"You need help," Mom said, her hands folded neatly in her lap. Her words felt scripted, as clinical as the crisp white shirt she had chosen for the occasion. Of all the people in my corner, Mom was the last one I expected to take the lead.

Howie cleared his throat and launched into a monologue about the dangers of continuing down my current path with pot, cocaine, and ecstasy. *How did he know?* I'd kept my double life far out of view of my teammates, mainly restricted to nights and weekends. I was dead wrong; someone had my number.

I vaguely recalled Marv's unheeded warning when I signed with the Raiders. He looked me straight in the eye once we were out of view of the cameras and explained, "Never, ever underestimate Al Davis. He'll do whatever it takes to protect his investments."

At the time, I nodded, thinking back to Coach Smith. His sources usually gave me up a day or two after a bender. But back then, nothing was caught on film, so plausible deniability ruled the day.

Like everything else, life was different now that I earned a hefty paycheck. With money and reputations on the line, the posse ripped the Band-Aid off fast. Despite being fully dressed, I suddenly felt naked, raw, and exposed. I could hear Tim's "deny, deny, deny" mantra pinballing around my head, but it was a tough audience. They operated as a united front, and any attempt to deny my addiction felt like bringing a spitball to a knife fight. I decided the best option was to roll over and fast.

I interrupted Howie, unable to contain my angst. "Stop, man. I'll do whatever you guys want. Just stop."

Howie's jaw twitched. Between his pit bull mandible and Marv's peaked eyebrows, I wanted it all to end.

The room went silent. Each person's expression, especially Howie's, reflected surprise mixed with relief. As for me, I suspect I still had a deer-in-the-headlights expression pasted on my face, but I needed to wake up from this nightmare. "Whatever it takes, I'll do it."

Mike cut in. He threw a verbal knife: "Rehab." He refused to give the word the cushion of a complete sentence. Meanwhile, Marv's lips closed tighter than a Ziploc.

"And if you don't finish, you don't play next year," Mike added, releasing the guillotine.

Another awkward silence overtook the space. I imagined a stay in a beach bungalow in Malibu. *Isn't that where most of the rehab clinics are in Los Angeles? I can handle that. Hell, maybe I can even get some surfing in while I'm there.*

As it turns out, I spent a month far from the beach at Rancho L'Abri, a secluded spot east of San Diego. Thank god it was isolated, because I dyed my hair, my eyebrows, and even my goatee jet black. If people didn't stare at me before, they sure as hell did after that makeover.

My first experience in rehab didn't alter my behavior one bit.

It only provided a brief interlude of clean living between phases of debauchery. Since I had the ego of a twenty-one-year-old, the therapy bounced off my armor, unable to penetrate my feeling of invincibility. A diagnosis of social anxiety was supposed to surprise me? Come on, I could've offered up that finding in high school. And sure, addiction ran in my family, but that wasn't my problem. I was a quarterback in the NFL; I couldn't be a junkie if I was operating at that high of a level, right? I was dead wrong, but my mind was a powerful weapon, and I wasn't ready to humble myself.

It didn't help that former Raiders who were my idols had survived similar reputations for unsavory off-field antics. Hell, the franchise was riddled with a history of misbehavior. The organization glorified antiestablishment conduct, and what could be more outside the norm than sniffing lines and throwing spirals?

My second rehab stint came in the spring of 1992, triggered by a call from the league office as a consequence of my positive result prior to the Kansas City game. By that afternoon, I had checked into the Betty Ford Center to stay until the staff deemed me ready. This round of treatment was deeply on the down-low—none of my teammates knew.

I was genuinely surprised by my test failure, because I'd conducted thorough research on undetectable drugs, namely acid. And alcohol should have been okay, too, assuming I stayed within limits. The tricky part about drinking was that I usually paired it with cocaine, which was a surefire way to fail. And forget about weed; that was a nonstarter. It was a slippery substance for me, while it was a nonissue for other addicts. Like many things in life, what worked for one might not work for others. Weed's role in recovery was so personal that people came up with a name for it: "California sobriety," meaning an addict was off all substances but weed. Given marijuana's widespread acceptance, that sounded reasonable, but not in my case. Sadly, it was one of the most insidious substances of them all. It spiraled me back to using everything else at my disposal.

So there I was, back in rehab for forty-five days. It was a record at the time, as most people only went to Betty Ford for thirty. As much as I wanted out, I performed well, becoming a five-star resident. Maybe it was the safe space or the daily structure. Whatever it was, I felt good, studied, and did the work.

There was another standout among the residents named Sam. He owned a tire shop nearby. We walked around Betty's lake most nights to kill the hours before curfew. He was a great guy and kept our strolls entertaining. Inevitably, we ended our nights talking about the well-fed bass in the lake. They were irresistible monsters. We fantasized about fishing, wondering how to get a rod through security. It seemed impossible to get something that obvious through the guards, so I chalked it up to a pipe dream.

Then, on my last night at the facility, Sam joined me for my final excursion around Betty's lake. But this time he approached with a sparkle in his eyes.

"Let's go," he said with uncharacteristic eagerness. "I've got two rods hidden by the lake."

"No shit." I punched his arm before grabbing my sweatshirt. "How the heck?"

Sam cut me off with a finger pressed to his dry lips.

"Okay. Let's go."

He flashed a shit-eating grin. "Perfect."

I spent my last night at the Betty Ford Center slaying fish under the desert sky with only the whizzing of reels filling the emptiness of night. By morning, we were back in bed, delightfully exhausted with some additional luggage. If it had been a Bassmaster tournament, I would've won with my best catch. I couldn't part with this behemoth, so when Mom picked me up, I concealed the king of all lake bass west of the Mississippi.

"What's that strange smell?" Mom asked, wrinkling her nose as I joined her in the car.

"A sizable gift from Betty," I said, unloading my prize possession from within the folds of my puffer jacket.

"Dear lord." She gawked and shook her head in disbelief as my nearly fifteen-pound largemouth bass approached her lips. "I believe that's Betty's $30,000 bass right there," she declared, and we both laughed so hard that she had to stop the car. What else could you do but find humor in the craziness of my life?

That night, we grilled Betty's bass in Mom's backyard and feasted as I vowed to remain clean and sober. That commitment held for a mere twenty-four hours, as by the next afternoon I was back at it, leaving a well-fed interlude of sobriety in my wake.

To be fair, Al and the Raiders coaching staff tried everything to rein me in, but nothing worked. They didn't understand addiction, and that was no hit on them: neither did I back then. Quitting wasn't a viable option. When given the decision to stop using or end my football career, I picked the latter every fricking time.

It turns out that Al Davis was fully aware of my unsanctioned activities. At my last meeting with Al, when he let me go after my third failed drug test, he offered a summary of my off-field activities. He knew where I went, who I associated with, and my drug preferences. He was all business but deeply disappointed too. Sitting in the armchair across from his desk, I watched Al lean forward on the table, resting on his elbows. He removed his glasses in a loosely controlled patience and stared directly into my throbbing eyes to ease the mounting tension.

"You tested positive again." Silence. "Todd, I've never been in this situation, and I hope I never will be again. But the NFL has your number." He paused, lifting a file stuffed with reports. "You're being suspended for a year." He stalled to emphasize his next point: "And the next positive is a blackball for life per NFL policy."

I nodded, unable to rearrange my problems to make them solvable. Addiction wasn't rational. I had to have drugs to survive life in the NFL, reaching the unenviable point of needing them more than football. Sure, I would miss my brothers in battle, the feeling of the ball in my hands, and the smell of the grass, but my positive feelings were limited to the field. On the flip side, I couldn't bear the near-daily urine testing, doubt, and relentless suspicion that cast a heavy shadow in the NFL's regimented world. More than anything else, I couldn't tolerate living under the league's thumb any longer. I felt nothing but relief as I looked past Al at the wall lined with coveted Raiders trophies, helmets, and photographs. None of it mattered anymore.

Al broke the quiet, clearing his throat. "So I won't pay you your third year of the contract. We're letting you go." Finally, I felt a touch of disappointment as I realized my honey hole was shutting down. Funding my lifestyle was about to get tricky. I didn't live large, but my habit was substantial. Yet this concern was a distant second to the comfort of knowing that the shackles were off.

This supposedly dream-worthy life was over. *What will I do now?* I had no idea, but it would involve an abundance of drugs.

Chapter Nine

A Headshot or a Mug Shot? The Grip of Addiction

I think hell is something you carry around with you. Not somewhere you go.

—Neil Gaiman

Was I an addict? As it turns out, I'd lied to myself as much as to the rest of the world. After leaving the Raiders, my denial and self-destruction reached deep into the abyss. I quieted my inner loathing with a range of drugs over the next three decades, including ecstasy, acid, cocaine, heroin, crack, and meth at deadly doses to disconnect from the misery inside. I didn't want to feel anything. While drugs didn't kill me, they dismantled the life I'd known for the past twenty-three years.

Staying in Los Angeles meant answering questions, chiefly "Are you going to play again?" I heard it in the streets when I was high, and it echoed in my dreams. Fans who'd stood in long lines for autographs in prior years sheltered their kids during encounters on the sidewalk. Their disgust amplified my negative self-talk and shredded any remaining self-worth. Even a call from the Pittsburgh Steelers expressing interest felt like a dull knife. That's when I knew I needed to leave town quickly.

Where does a six-foot-five-inch orange-haired guy hide out in euphoric misery? Unwilling to answer to anyone, I completely lost touch with my internal compass. I packed up the Land Cruiser, loaded a longboard on the roof, grabbed a few of my boys, and headed toward Mexico for a period of temporary death. It was sizzling, hotter than Hades even under the trees, but I didn't mind. No one cared who I was or what I did down south. "Hey gringo" was my call sign, and that was perfectly fine with me. I was there but not present.

While friends came and went, my pattern was predictable: drugs, surf, food, more substances, and intermittent sleep in my ride. Drugs consumed an inordinate amount of my daily cycle, from procurement to their aftermath. I wasn't partying in the glorified sense. I was slowly dying by suicide. Addiction was anything but blissful. It forced vigilance or I risked a crushing withdrawal—negative reinforcement at its finest.

More than any other drug, heroin in all its forms changed my life. It also bled me dry. By 1994, funds had run dangerously low as I went everywhere to go nowhere. I was desperate. What does a college dropout do to make fast cash? Go with a known trade: football. On my return to California, an epiphany struck. The Canadian Football League (CFL) didn't test for drugs. *Hell, yes.*

I packed my bags for Canada to join the Winnipeg Blue Bombers in 1994.

Things were different in the CFL, and I was different too. It wasn't about football anymore. I needed a paycheck to inject it into my right arm. Yet my first run in the league didn't last long. I blew out my knee on the opening day of training camp. This short stint, however, charted the path for my return to the British Columbia Lions in 1999.

But before returning to football, I needed to rehabilitate my bum knee. I was in no hurry to return, so I took my time. About two years later, when the acute part of my recovery was in the rearview mirror, I rediscovered a favorite stress reliever: pickup basketball by the beach in Orange County under the setting sun. It was therapeutic in many regards, except for one night in 1997 that took a very dark turn. The game was an equal matchup with plenty of gentle ribbing until my 275-pound buddy took it a step too far. His exaggerated dunk landed him flat on his back, like a sweaty, oversized human pancake. He couldn't walk off the court, so some of us dragged him back to my place. Everyone hoped rest might be the solution.

"I'm in rough shape, man. Got anything for the pain?" he pleaded, struggling to get comfortable on the couch. He could barely wipe the sweat from the puddles under his eyes.

I paused, taking a quick mental inventory of my medications. Advil wouldn't put a dent in his pain. There was my stash of the good stuff, but that might be too much for him. *I'm pretty sure that they use fentanyl in hospitals, but heroin?*

"I've got something that would work." I hesitated before explaining further. "But it's not over-the-counter stuff," I admitted, looking him directly in the eyes.

"As long as it works, I don't care," he confirmed, still wincing in pain.

"Okay then, I got you." I headed to the bathroom to grab my kit. I closed the door. I didn't want any of my buddies watching me cook a fix, followed by a small syringe for the patient. He was no lightweight, but even a few drops could be a tsunami to his system. So I settled on a quarter dose of black tar heroin before hiding my stash in its usual spot.

I approached with the needle. He snickered. "Doctor Todd, now that's a first. You are either my savior or the Grim Reaper. I can't decide."

His words would resonate later, given what was about to transpire, but we had no way of knowing that yet. I was too busy indulging in the bliss and relaxation that accompanied a high. "I got you. No worries, brother."

His arms were straight-up nurse porn, veins bulging due to low body fat, so I didn't bother with a tourniquet.

"I'd look away," I suggested.

He started to squirm. "Okay," he agreed, resting his gaze on the crew jacking around in the kitchen.

After administering relief, I headed to the porch for a smoke. I'd give him about ten minutes to settle in, then check on the pain.

When I finished, my guys were raiding the cupboards like rummaging raccoons. I turned to see my friend either sleeping or . . . wait a minute. His chest barely rose. Something was wrong—very wrong. As I approached, I noticed foam lining the edges of his mouth. I panicked, yelling for the guys in the kitchen.

"Help me get him to the shower," I shouted as I slapped his

cheeks, trying in vain to revive him. His lids weren't reacting. His breathing was sporadic.

"We could barely move him the first time. There's got to be another way," one of my guys stated while bits of a Pop-Tart flew from his mouth.

"Stay with him," I ordered, running out to the lawn to grab a garden hose. I dragged it in and blasted him in the face along with my living room wall, but he still didn't respond. One more blast, hosing his face and upper torso—still nothing.

"Fuckkkkkk," I yelled, realizing 911 was the only viable option.

When I got the operator on the line, my buddies, who were now fully aware of my misstep, vanished. They didn't want anything to do with the shit show.

"911, what is the nature of your emergency?" A woman's voice sounded clear and ready to help.

"My buddy isn't breathing. He's foaming at the mouth. Have them come quick," I commanded in a disjointed panic.

"Sir, you need to start CPR," she responded calmly. "Can you tell me what happened while you begin compressions?"

"Umm, not really," I hedged, refusing to admit my mistake. Then I paused, looked at my friend, and reeled in my fears. "I think he overdosed," I confessed.

"Okay, I dispatched an ambulance and the police," she stated. "Now, do you know how to administer CPR?"

Another embarrassing admission followed; I couldn't bring myself to do it—the crisis had stalled my mind. She walked me through the steps. After a round or two, I got in a rhythm, and within minutes the ambulance and cops arrived.

Relief flooded through me as the professionals entered the

soggy living room. With bodies flooding the space, it turned into an unsolved crime scene. By the time they readied the gurney, things seemed more under control, with my buddy breathing unassisted. But the tension came rushing back as the cops started searching my place. I knew my hiding spot was solid, yet the boys in blue took their time. They didn't come up empty-handed. The duck-footed sheriff's deputy emerged from the garage with a grin and a garbage bag of marijuana trimmings.

"Do you want to explain these, Marijuana-vich?" His lips curled.

My reputation preceded me. *Deny, deny, deny.* "No idea," I stated for the record. It was half true; I had no idea they'd find the trimmings. I got them from a farm inland, but that location would go to my grave.

Then the cop's more pigeon-toed and overweight sidekick emerged from my laundry room with two half-dead plants dangling from his hands. "You know it's a felony to cultivate marijuana, right?" the pock-faced mutt asked.

To add insult to injury, the paramedics handed the cops the emptied syringe on their way out, along with a prescription bottle of pills in someone else's name—more for the growing list of charges.

I shook my head, rose, and placed my hands behind my back to get it over quickly. "Let's go." I was sick of the banter.

The whole ordeal landed me two months in the Orange County Jail in Santa Ana, California, a hellscape housing every social disease imaginable. I wilted without natural sunlight in a building that should've been condemned. Then they moved me to the James A. Musick Facility, aka "the Honor Farm," a minimum-security center. In an ironic twist, it was named after former NFL running back James Musick, who worked as a deputy for the Orange County Sheriff's Department in the offseason.

This move was a blessing, offering me ample time outside. I did nearly every job available, including picking vegetables, tending to the chickens, mending pipes, and even serving as an umpire for softball games. My favorite was the irrigation work, since I got to soak in the sunlight while munching on everything from lettuce to broccoli. If I had to be incarcerated, it was about as good as it could get.

Despite my growing record, a few NFL teams showed interest in the spring of 1999 after I was cleared to reenter the NFL. I trained hard and fast in preparation for workouts with the Seattle Seahawks, who met with me in Los Angeles. Next came the Chargers in San Diego with Coach Mike Riley, a former assistant head coach at USC. This was followed by the Chicago Bears, the most promising franchise, who liked what they saw during a strong workout at their facility. The coaches seemed very interested until a fateful medical clearance physical.

"Keep your toes pointing skyward," the doctor instructed, gnawing on a sizable wad of gum. That stinky tropical flavor that smelled worse than sunscreen triggered a wave of nausea—a foreboding sign.

"Okay," I said, not looking down as I fiddled with a roll of athletic tape.

"To the sky," he reiterated.

"I am." Irritation changed the timbre of my voice. I looked down at his furrowed brow.

He tapped my left foot with his instrument and grunted. "Well, then there's a problem here, son. Your left foot is floppy."

"Floppy?" I repeated, understanding the sciatic pain that shot down my leg was anything but random. It was worse than the aftermath of back-to-back games. The pain had started two weeks prior when I wrecked my back playing pickup basketball. It was horrible timing for a pump fake gone wrong, but I hoped to breeze through the physical since the rest of me was in solid shape.

"Huh?" I leaned on my elbows, shooting him the "you're crazy" face.

"Any problems with your back?" he asked, looking up.

"Not really," I hedged. *Oh man.* I knew this was the end of the line. I fell silent. By this point, managing my anxiety was a full-time job.

"Okay, that's enough for today," he said apologetically as he obsessed over his clipboard.

I knew exactly what came next: a letter citing medical ineligibility. I'd pivot until my herniated disk healed. So I returned to Canada to dress as a backup quarterback for eighteen games, never taking a snap.

My season with the BC Lions in 1999 was one of the darkest years of my life. Sure, it was an idyllic setting where the Rockies met the Pacific Ocean, but I overlooked the natural wonders. Instead, I locked myself in a sardine-can-sized apartment in the city of White Rock, British Columbia, making trips to the needle exchange once a week for a fresh pack of fifty syringes. I wasn't alone; the drug epidemic in neighboring Vancouver was creeping toward its zenith. Meanwhile, I began a love affair with the insanely potent China White.

Don't let the name fool you. China White was anything but pure. In highbrow circles, they called it a "designer opioid," but that's too kind. In truth, it was a gritty back-alley mainstay. In most instances, it was a mixture of fentanyl with residues of heroin or even cocaine. Without regulation, it was anyone's guess. What I know with absolute certainty: the shit was no joke. When you think hard-core, China White was at the top of the list, a hundred times more potent than heroin, morphine, or fentanyl. In my experience, the high lasted longer, explaining the vast appeal.

As implausible as it sounds, I showed up at practices and games high on this garbage. And the pangs of withdrawal were indiscriminate, once kicking in during a midseason matchup. My bones ached, and my mind couldn't focus on anything but a fix. At halftime, I grabbed my kit and hurried to the bathroom stalls to silence the pain.

As I lit the pipe, a full-throated Coach Greg Mohns engaged me from the other side of the wall. "Todd, what do you think about that last running play from your vantage point?"

"Looked good to me, Coach," I answered, fumbling with the pipe. It was a silly question, given that I'd stood on the sideline taking it all in, just like him.

"Exactly. We need to run that one again," he announced with vigor.

In a panic to finish, I dropped the pipe and sliced my thumb, emerging with a wad of toilet paper encasing my hand.

"What the heck?" the tight end asked.

"Don't ask," I said, laughing it off. Everyone but lineman Mohammed Elewonibi moved on. Mo paused, looked me straight in the eyes, and winced. I nodded awkwardly, longing to hide. *He's onto me. Jesus Christ, this is a new low.*

High and injured, I took my spot on the bench to ride it out. Without the drugs, I couldn't make it through the game. And without the game check, I couldn't secure more. The vicious cycle felt unstoppable as I wasted away into a puddle of bones at 176 pounds.

How did I survive? I'd be in a shallow grave on the edge of town if not for Mo. This winner of the Outland Trophy, awarded to the best college football interior lineman, played in the NFL for the Redskins and Eagles before electing to complete his career in British Columbia. Originally from Nigeria, he was raised in the Vancouver suburbs as the quintessential kind Canadian.

Not long after the season ended, Mo appeared on my porch with a clear directive. "Todd, let me in. I'm taking you home, buddy."

I had no sense of time, but by the looks of the syringe on the far side of the bed, I'd spent the last twelve hours riding the China White express train to nowhere. "Give me a minute," I hollered, unprepared to share my squalor with anyone, much less a teammate.

Mo read my mind. "I don't give a shit about your place, man, just open the damn door now. It's fricking cold out here."

"Okay, okay," I shouted, grabbing my board shorts and heading his way. A blast of Siberian-style air hit like a hard slap as I opened the rickety door. Mo stood there with two suitcases and a look of determination.

"What the heck," I said, bleary-eyed and perplexed.

"You need to get out of here," he declared. "Get your stuff and your dog. I'm driving you back to California now."

Honestly, I couldn't think of a constructive reason not to go. I looked him in the eye, smiled for the first time in weeks, and nodded in agreement. "Home," I mouthed, confirming the plan. I couldn't resist. It felt like the right thing to do. Well, that was until we were several cities into a twenty-two-hour drive. The withdrawals were relentless as my body revolted: puking, shaking, and writhing in agony. Addiction proved to be less about gratification and more about escaping pain.

This idea that junkies were hedonic pleasure-seekers was a crock of shit. By the time we hit Portland, I wanted to die. If there'd been a handgun nearby, I would've put it in my mouth to end the misery. Never before or since have I experienced anguish on that scale.

"I can't do this, Mo. I can't make it without a hit." I squirmed in the seat. My bones ached from the inside out, radiating from the marrow.

Mo was unflappable. "It's not a choice. You have to, Todd. You won't make it otherwise," he said with wisdom beyond his years.

"I'd rather die." It hung in the air for a few seconds with a heaviness that hit Mo hard. Why? Because he knew I meant it. Mo gazed out the window, refusing to respond.

"You will thank me someday," he said with firm but unmistakable care. He was right. I'd thank him a million times for saving my life that day. I was Mo's first unofficial patient. He became a renowned addiction counselor on Vancouver Island after retirement from football.

Mo joined me in battle on the field and off, like many other teammates who watched out for me over the years. It was a reminder that the pain and intensity that bonded us in football lasted a lifetime. Yet, even with this unconditional support during different phases of my journey, I was still a runaway locomotive.

Next came an expansion team in the arena league, the Los Angeles Avengers, in 2000. Holy shit, I thought it couldn't get any worse than my experience in British Columbia. I could sum up the whole experience in two words: dope sick. I was at my all-time low in Houston while using a favorite: black tar heroin, which is as dirty as it sounds, but with the rush of ten simultaneous orgasms that left me feeling like I was in the womb. This variant, also known as black dragon, was sticky like tar. The consistency was a result of crude processing that left behind plenty of impurities. But by that point, I didn't care about contamination as I occasionally added crack into my drug regimen. My system was a messy cocktail well beyond repair. As long as it got me high, I was in. And since needles were harder to come by in Los Angeles and Orange County than in Vancouver, I resorted to a pipe to get my fix.

The trip to Houston was particularly rough because instead of my usual chaperone to keep me in check, I brought my pipe. Continuing my death march, I got high when I checked into my room, not concerned with the consequences or the drug's lingering effects on my body. I received a harsh reminder during the game the next day.

I suited up in white and had my first accident before kickoff. A word to the wise: never wear bright white, especially when you lose all control of your bodily functions on heroin. That's right, I shit my fricking pants. But not just once. I changed my pants four times that day. Fortunately, Coach Stan Brock, a former NFL tackle, didn't ask questions.

Time stopped during that game. I swore the action dragged on forever as I fought to keep myself together. After the third change of pants, the equipment guy leaned in. "Todd, that's your second-to-last pair; keep it together, man."

I nodded with zero confidence that I could deliver.

At halftime, I hustled into the locker room to peer in the

mirror: Constricted pinpoint pupils, check. Diarrhea, most definitely check. Vomiting? Not yet. *Maybe I took it a wee bit too far last night?*

At the end of halftime, I cornered my backup, begging him to be ready for action. Then I noticed Coach Brock watching from afar. I reined it in fast, as this was a surefire way to get on his shit list. No matter the personal cost, I'd have to finish the second half.

It was a dirty game in more ways than one, but somehow I managed to throw ten touchdowns. You read that right; it was my record. Yet the game still resulted in a disappointing loss. My performance did, however, prove that I was an excellent fit for the arena league. My quick touch passes were perfect for the fast-paced game. Who knows what might have been if I'd sobered up?

Despite my physical condition, I made the all-rookie team. I had 168 completions for 296 passes with 45 touchdowns and 9 picks. Not shabby for a raging junkie. Was I aware of how bad things were? Of course, but I couldn't rein it in; that's the irony of addiction. No matter what I understood, it wouldn't stop me.

Not long after the Houston debacle, X-Man, the trusted security guard from my USC days, worked behind the scenes to get me help. He tapped Garo Ghazarian, an attorney and professor at USC. I didn't show up to practice the first time Garo came by, but he returned undeterred. He knew my struggles, as he'd overcome his own. After growing up in Beirut, Lebanon, he made it to Los Angeles only to lose it all to crack cocaine. Garo recovered and understood what it took to fight addiction: persistence. He showed up again at practice the next day. By the end of the week, I'd moved in with his family, nestled in Little Armenia in

Glendale, California. And so the list of people coming to my aid grew in lockstep with my addiction.

Before the next Avengers season, the team named me the franchise player, an honor that came with a decent check. And what did I do with the influx of $30,000? The cops arrested me for heroin possession at the team facility. Surprised? You shouldn't be.

My record was inconsistent on and off the field, but then came one claim that wasn't in the same orbit: an accusation of sexual assault. While I wasn't above hurting myself, I couldn't intentionally inflict pain on someone else. Never. Looking back on all the difficult times in my life, I can attest that I refused to get physical with anyone off the field. It wasn't in my nature. I was more inclined to remove myself from a situation than to allow it to escalate to violence.

I replayed the night so many times in my head, struggling to understand the woman's about-face after what I felt was an innocent hookup. Nothing explained the events the next day, when I was removed from the Avengers' locker room in handcuffs. I was floored. My first call from the Marina del Rey Sheriff's Department was not to a lawyer but to the only woman on my mind.

"Hi, Gramma, it's Todd."

"Hi, honey. Well, this is a pleasant surprise." I could tell from her voice that I'd just made her day. I hated what I had to do next.

"I just want you to know that you will see some things on the local news tonight that aren't true."

"Oh, dear, okay." I heard her fishing for the remote control to turn down *Good Morning America*. Then things went quiet on her end.

"I need you to know that none of it is true."

"Of course, honey. I've known for a long time that the media is just as eager to tear you down as build you up."

"That's right, but know I'll get it sorted out."

"Okay, honey. Now go do what needs to be done."

"Thanks, Gramma, that's exactly what I am about to do. I love you." I hung up with an ache in my heart. I wanted to spare my entire family from a flogging in the ill-informed court of public opinion, but I couldn't. I felt utterly helpless, a feeling that gave me great compassion for the falsely accused.

In my police statement, I explained what I felt was the consensual nature of the night. I had about seven people over to my place—all lit and hanging in the living room. We exchanged flirty eyes, and one of the women joined me in the bedroom. It was your garden-variety sex, nothing crazy or noteworthy. The rest of the crew, including several of her girlfriends, were one thin wall away in the living room, well within earshot. There was never a "no," "stop," or anything of the sort. The accusation made no sense to me. The district attorney's office didn't file charges, but it was an ordeal that I never fully understood.

The Avengers stuck by me through it all, even though I was a ghost during the offseason workouts and the first part of training camp. There was no getting around the mandated yearlong stay in a treatment facility following a felony heroin possession. Then my second season was anything but stellar, as my drug use never hit a glass ceiling. On the field, I went 81 for 176 with 17 touchdowns and 12 interceptions, along with a few game ejections for throwing a clipboard and hand towel at referees. Whoops. Eventually, the staff had seen enough and suspended me for conduct detrimental to the team. They couldn't bring themselves to tell the truth: keeping an unpredictable junkie on the payroll was an accident waiting to happen.

I was flat broke by the start of 2004, when ESPN listed me as one of the twenty-five biggest sports flops in history—as if I needed a reminder that my life had spiraled. I lived in my Chevy Astro van, a drug-laden jalopy that was quite an eyesore on the family-friendly Balboa Peninsula. Time was fluid as I wasted the days scoring drugs and wandering the beach—that is, until I lost my license and then my ride. Without a space of my own, I migrated to couch surfing with family and friends, using a skateboard for transportation. Mom's house was a respite for food and a shower at first, but eventually she was advised to turn me away. It nearly killed her to rebuff her son, but even though she'd served as a safe harbor for decades, she couldn't save me. As for Marv, I kept my distance during the height of my addiction. Any remaining shards of my pride prevented me from showing up on his doorstep.

After a few months, the last of my family and friends refused to watch me self-destruct and moved me along. I never misbehaved or stole belongings for drugs, contrary to the occasional accusation of a five-finger discount. But the whole scene was too much for my hosts to wrap their minds around. If I'd had a missing limb, they might have been compassionate, but the invisible condition of addiction, much like mental illness, was too intangible and scary. I was extremely sick, but it wasn't something to bandage and heal. So I suffered silently, treated as little more than a nuisance. Kurt Cobain's famous line was certainly true in my case: "If my eyes could show my soul, everyone would cry when they saw me smile."

Homeless and practically penniless, I turned to the cheapest drug I could find: meth, a cortisone shot to the subcortex. I smoked, snorted, injected, and swallowed it—whatever it took. On a perpetual high, I surfed on concrete, spending my days wheeling in an endless pursuit of unreachable peace. It was a fragment of an existence that had to end, but how or when was anyone's guess.

There was nothing like trying to elude the cops on a skateboard at age thirty-five to remind me where things stood before my fifth arrest. As with most days, I ignored signs and skated through a prohibited zone. The moment I entered, the cops were in pursuit. The meth and syringes got me sent straight to jail for eighteen days, followed by several weeks of probation. By this point, I had been incarcerated so often that the jail played dedicated walk-in music: "Welcome Back," the Kotter theme song; and "The Autumn Wind," the Raiders' signature music. Then I was back again in May 2005, after a painful and even more public episode where I solidified my reputation as a runner.

Not surprisingly, it all started with skateboarding in a prohibited zone. The cops locked in and chased me onto the boardwalk, where I abandoned my ride and grabbed a rogue beach cruiser. I pulled off the main strip, weaving through the back alleys of my youth. I knew those streets better than any cop in town. Think O. J. Simpson, but on a Huffy, knitting my way through alley dumpsters instead of cars on the 405 Freeway. After fifteen blocks, they ate my dust, so I juked back onto the boardwalk and bailed out for a sprint to the beach bathhouse. I didn't dare slow down to look back and lose my impressive lead, so I slid into a stall and hopped onto the toilet to wait them out.

"We know you're in here, Marinovich," I heard a voice bellow.

"Come out with your hands up," another voice demanded.

I didn't move a muscle, crouching and panting louder than a wild dog.

"Jesus Christ, Todd, get the fuck out here."

Wait a minute. *Who the hell?* I stopped breathing briefly as my mind raced through its primitive identification system. I drew a blank, but the spinning in my head continued.

Footsteps approached, followed by a firm rap on the other stalls as he came down the line. "I mean it, Todd."

That voice again. *Why does it sound familiar?*

A body rounded the corner and I stared straight ahead, locking eyes with a classmate from high school. *Holy shit.*

"No fucking way," I said in disbelief.

"No more bullshit, Todd. This is serious."

"It wouldn't be if you'd just leave me the fuck alone." I stepped down with my hands up.

"There are no words . . ." my classmate muttered. "This would be funny if it wasn't so sad," he stated, looking away.

"Yup, I've heard it all before. Save your breath," I snapped. I hated being treated like a leper.

He stepped away, and one of the other cops patted me down, uncovering my kit with meth and loose syringes. At the station, I heard my walk-on music again, followed by a few chuckles from some graybeards. This time, I wasn't in the mood for others laughing at my expense, so I inked my occupation as "artist and anarchist."

Fuck you all.

Between the drugs, the paraphernalia, and resisting arrest, it didn't look good. With my extensive record, I had two options: return to jail or go to drug treatment on my dime. I couldn't shell out that kind of coin, so jail seemed imminent. News of my predicament spread fast through the USC network. Twenty-three teammates pooled the funds to pay for my treatment. To suggest I was blown away would be a gross understatement. I wouldn't have expected this support in a million years, nor did I feel deserving.

I desperately wanted to get clean out of respect for my boys, but the grip of addiction was impossible to shake. The chronic use of drugs had altered my dopamine threshold, and the cravings were too much to bear. So, in September 2005, I walked out of the residential treatment program in clear violation of my sentence. I was on the run for weeks before the cops tracked me down and hauled me back to jail with another felony possession charge. Cue the Kotter theme music. Hell, at this rate, keep it playing. I managed to get this last charge dismissed in exchange for completing a sixty-day court-mandated program, but all it did was dredge up overwhelming guilt and shame.

A subsequent arrest in August 2007 started with another cruise through a prohibited area in the west oceanfront parking lot in Newport Beach. I took off on a skateboard while clutching my guitar case in another futile attempt to evade the cops. After a few blocks, I ditched my goods and pressed ahead on foot. At one point, a cop had me cornered. I froze, debating my dwindling options.

"Don't make me do it, Todd," the cop shouted.

What is "it"? And how does this guy know me, too? As it turns out, they all recognized me by this point. My drug use was an open secret.

I pivoted, about to sprint away, when he reached to his hip. I was startled by a popping sound. Pain shot through my lower back and legs, followed by an uncontrollable spasm. The cop had tased me, but he didn't stop me. I slid through an open complex door and bolted up a back stairwell to a second-floor balcony. When a light came on, I saw a man open his patio door. He peered out my way and slammed it shut. No one would help. I couldn't blame them.

As I raced around the balcony, I heard a helicopter and saw a spotlight piercing the night sky. Then the sound of dogs barking intensified as they zeroed in on my location. There was no escaping. Once a police dog came into clear view, I dropped to the ground. I wouldn't risk getting torn to pieces by a Buster look-alike, followed by a lengthy prison sentence. Things were bad enough already.

I spread my arms and legs and begged the cop to pull back the canine. Thankfully, he showed some compassion. Another cop following my trail confiscated the discarded guitar case containing meth and syringes. I was charged with another felony drug possession and, in what was by now a predictable pattern, resisting arrest. This time, the court system didn't show restraint. I was sentenced to a full year in treatment and five years of probation.

This forced year of sobriety was a gift. From 2007 to 2008, I worked with national drug and alcohol treatment centers in Newport Beach, helping others overcome addiction. While I was far from an expert, supporting teammates in battle was second nature. I was on the right track, and leaders in the recovery space took notice. Hired as a lecturer by Newport Coast Recovery, I felt good to be making a difference and bringing something positive into the world. Finally, the distraction of my mess wasn't taking away from my message. But then I was arrested on April 4, 2009, for failing to appear at a progress review appointment. So I landed back in jail and then into a court program designed for multiple offenders.

The program was different, though. This was where I met my

future wife, Alix. She understood my agony as much as her own. From the moment we met, I knew we could build something beautiful out of our pain. But Alix rejected me the first time I asked her out. It went against the rules of the program. However, I didn't give up. Eventually, we married and welcomed our son, Baron, that same year. But as his birth approached, I struggled to stay clean. With support and encouragement from Alix, I turned myself in for relapsing. My wife and son deserved better, and I fought like hell to give it to them, leaving the program briefly for his birth. Holding him during those early moments, I knew that I was meant to be a dad—my greatest joy.

The following year, I faced an unspeakable tragedy that rocked me to the core. Marco Coski Forster, my ride-or-die, overdosed on heroin. Marco had been clean for nine years, yet addiction proved a patient disease, awaiting complacency. This loss was beyond my comprehension, leading me to question sobriety altogether. *Am I living under a false sense of security? If it took Marco, what could happen to me?* I resisted these thoughts as I welcomed our daughter in July 2011, naming her Coski in honor of my remarkable friend. A spirited, loving light known as Coco, she embodies all the good in Marco and more.

Amid the highs and lows less than a decade into the new millennium, ESPN filmed *The Marinovich Project*. It should've been a dream effort, but I had a tough time keeping it together off camera. During the filming, I had to put on the facade that I was in recovery. I couldn't afford for anyone to find out that I was chipping, meaning not in the depths of addiction but far from clean. Well versed in lying, I fooled everyone but myself while the documentary received high praise. It was a great story, just not entirely mine.

During this period, I got by with help from family while scraping barnacles off yachts for forty dollars a boat, a far cry from a multimillion-dollar NFL package. I didn't care, though. I had to keep my mind and body busy so that I wouldn't succumb to drugs. I also taught art at a local community center, which led to commissioned work.

I painted a mural in Garden Grove, California. The place had a reputation, but so did I. With the city's help, I created something beautiful, my most significant work to date because so many people could experience and enjoy it.

My mural in Garden Grove, California, in 2014.

While my marriage to Alix didn't survive this period of intermittent sobriety, we made parenting work, with the kids living with her in Orange County during the school year and with me on weekends and most summers, unless I was in "Dadda School," our code for treatment. Then came another unfortunate turn of events that rightfully blew up my path.

August 19, 2016, was a night that, no matter what I do, I can't erase from my memory. It was the most humiliating experience of a long list of follies. It wasn't a backyard naked drug romp as the media suggested, at least from my vantage point at the time. It all felt entirely rational in my haze. I was on a skateboard during a summer heat wave in Irvine, California, with the temperatures cresting over ninety degrees. Looking for a pool to escape the heat, I spied one identical to my in-laws'. They lived in Los Angeles, but I was convinced it was their pool. I let myself in through the gate, and because I didn't have a bathing suit, I prepared to swim in the buff. Again, it was all reasonable in my altered mind since no one was in sight. Perched against the pool's edge with elbows by my sides, I looked up at the night sky to enjoy the peace and stillness. Then I dozed off.

A creaking sound and a pop of light from the balcony above startled me to attention. A spotlight illuminated my naked body, followed by a high-pitched scream, something from a Hitchcock movie, not a cul-de-sac. Before I could rise to my feet, five police officers surrounded me, squawking to "stop resisting arrest."

"I'm fucking naked, bro, I'm not resisting shit," I insisted. By this point, I'd seen enough horror movies to know they came in various forms. The cops cuffed me in the buff and dragged me to the squad car. Papa had to be rolling over in his grave at this cringeworthy moment.

I was charged with trespassing, public nudity, and drug possession. It shocked me back to reality. In the aftermath, I had plenty of time to think. No one came to bail me out of jail the following day; I was rightfully alone. And since the cops had arrested me without clothes, I suffered the indignity of walking seven miles in a paper suit upon release. On the long walk, I thought about my losing battle. Even with the powerful motivation of my kids, I still wasn't successful. Nothing could outlove my pain. That realization was truly devastating.

How many times have I been to rehab? The god's honest truth: I'd lost count after seven. And each time, I'd believed with all my heart that it was my last. Did it work? In many ways, yes. I wouldn't be alive without those professionals, but the real work happened after I walked out their doors.

I was ready to make a life change when I arrived at Mom's house at noon the next day. I saw the desperation in her eyes. Then I saw it in my own. It was time to wage a daily resistance against the most formidable enemy of my life: addiction.

Chapter Ten

Art and Recovery

My truth and my lie met on the same day: I was an addict and I could handle it. It was hard to talk about and difficult to reach that deep, but I needed to break through to a life worth living. I had a superpower in my corner: if I applied the same near-radical passion for football and drugs to my recovery, anything was possible.

And I was not alone. One man in this world shared my power: Buzzy. He'd been there all along, in his way, since my first cry. Buried under a dumpster fire of misguided but unwavering love, he was my throughline. One of the worst sports fathers in history? Not a chance. ESPN, *Sports Illustrated*, and others got it all wrong. The media failed to capture how much I sought time with my hero. And toward the end of his life, Buzzy helped me recover the person I was meant to be; he was never judging and always loving.

Yes, Buzzy was Marv Marinovich. He emerged from the same body but had a different spirit entirely. Buzzy was Marv's alter ego, a potent mixture of joy and love, who turned the sunset years of our relationship into something I treasured. His eyes softened, his body relaxed, and his heart opened wider.

We were already deeply bonded, and art reinforced our connectedness. During the last few years of Buzzy's life, he lived with me in Orange County for long stints. By this point, his Alzheimer's was hard to ignore. I couldn't leave him alone. I bathed him, made his morning breakfast, and ensured he brushed his teeth—a remarkable reversal of roles. I felt it was a gift to give back to the man who'd offered me so much.

We worked in solidarity by day, Buzzy sanding his whiskey-colored wood sculpture while I painted in the shed, always within earshot. Then, once Buzzy fell asleep after dinner, I worked into the early-morning hours, refining his creations or my own. He was a natural. He could've been a successful sculptor if he'd chosen that path, following the family bloodline: my great-grandmother Nell Brink was an accomplished painter.

"I think it's worth sharing with the world," I said one night as Buzzy wrapped up his efforts nearly sixteen months into the project. He didn't make eye contact, just scanned the massive sculpture with his eye for detail as the dust settled.

I gave him ample time to ponder the proposition as he scrutinized every foot the way he used to analyze athletes. He was measured, but I knew his tells well. His calm demeanor meant intense contemplation or pride so overwhelming that he needed time to select his words. He responded with a nearly inaudible grunt and nod before wadding his sandpaper. That was code for yes, a modest but definite yes.

Then, without warning, he looked me straight in the eyes and remarked, "This is good. We're good." He didn't have to explain. I knew.

I smiled with a full-face expression that wrinkled every divot of my well-worn face. I wiped my lids as my tear ducts revealed a fountain of emotion. "Yeah, Buzzy, we're more than good." I grabbed his hand, sandpaper and all, and squeezed it gently. "I love you," I said without reservation.

He nodded, peered back at our creation, and shuffled toward the screen door.

I watched him move, physically a shell of his former self but with a heart now stronger than any other muscle. His exterior deterioration was difficult to watch, but the expression of his better being was the unexpected reward.

I made our usual that night: pan-seared chicken breasts with brown rice and vegetables. It was one of our better meals, maybe because I knew few remained. We sat at a flimsy dining set bought at a local flea market like most of my patchwork of essentials. The place was our little sanctuary, a new kind of dojo—this time dedicated to the arts.

I could feel everything unsaid as we ate in silence with an unmistakable knowing: our bond extended beyond the limitations of life. Everything was more than good. We were both alive to enjoy the long arc of our relationship, playing a profound role in each other's story.

That night, I fell into an active dream sequence. It was a journey back in time to answer a lingering question: Was I an artist or athlete first? I knew in my heart, but retracing early steps offered more clues.

It was my fourth birthday, and I was jogging four miles at a steady clip, my little legs taking four strides for every one of Marv's. I knew because I couldn't count above five yet. The air rushed from my tiny lungs. It raced for an escape so I could pull in the new. Every in-breath made me feel human again. The air was salty, but beggars couldn't be choosers. Tiny beads of sweat formed on my forehead. There would be more as I fought to keep up with Marv on the beach run.

He pulled ahead, not going easy on anyone, especially me. The Balboa Pier was in sight. I fixated on the columns. When I finally made it there, touching the smooth, weather-worn wood before heading back, Marv smiled approvingly. My insides warmed with pride. I'd do just about anything for his attention.

Advancing a year, I was with Traci and her friends for a dress-up session in their imaginary shop. They named me Molly, maybe so the presence of a boy seemed less obvious.

"Try this on," declared Traci, tossing me a tutu and a ball gown. Cakey blue eye shadow sprinkled from her lids onto her cheeks. But the mess was less distracting than the rogue lines of Mom's expired peach lipstick. Traci looked like a Picasso-inspired print. I stifled my giggles.

"I can't wear both," I decided, familiar enough with women's clothing to know this was a step too far.

"Oh yes you can, Molly. It's our dress shop," she stated, pointing to her girlfriends, who were also jury members. The subtext was clear: get with the plan or leave the shop.

I loved this game, so I got on board, slipping into the ballgown and shimmying the pink tutu over the long, silky blue fabric. I spun for the crowd. They smiled with approval, so I took my show on the road.

I twirled through the kitchen to regale Mom while she chatted on the phone. She shot me a big smile, put her hand over the receiver, and offered a sly whistle. Then she whispered, "Dad's home in a half hour," before returning to her conversation.

She didn't need to elaborate. I wasn't going to let him catch me in a tutu.

I also spent endless hours playing with Mom's and Traci's hair in the living room, my Vidal Sassoon studio. My focus was unmistakable as I designed their coifs, fine-tuned their bangs, and created beautiful cascading waves. I was so passionate about the craft that I declared my future as a hairdresser in front of Marv one night. Mom smiled, Traci ignored me, and Marv almost fell out of his chair. He howled, laughing so hard that he cried, tears streaming down his face as he grabbed his side, aching in laughter. "Keep dreaming, Red Rocket."

I don't remember my response, but Marv's reaction lodged deep in my subconscious. I focused on my work, pretending not to hear as I adjusted Mom's Lynda Carter–inspired locks.

Then I was in preschool, losing track of time doodling and drawing, fully immersed in my designs. I was glued to the chair. Nothing else generated this level of focus. While recess was fun, it didn't fill my cup the same way. But then organized sports entered the scene in elementary school. They were all-consuming and Marv encouraged me, seeing something that I didn't yet recognize.

Between football, basketball, and track, there was little time left for art in the evenings. And so it took a back seat. Marv didn't deliberately or maliciously neglect my creative pursuits; there simply weren't enough hours in a day. I tucked the paint and sketchbook away in the cavernous closet so I could join Marv in the dojo.

When I woke from my dream in the house I shared with Buzzy, I had my answer. As Phylicia Rashad wisely explained, "Before a child speaks, it sings. Before they write, they paint. As soon as they stand, they dance. Art is the basis of human expression."

In my case, it all came full circle. Over thirty years later, when I finally got comfortable in my artistic skin, these early loves married to produce something special. It started when former Raiders president Marc Badain approached me about painting the future Raiders stadium planned for Las Vegas. It would be a birthday gift for owner Mark Davis. I jumped at the chance.

That offering led to commissioned work for the franchise, including paintings of past Raiders facilities. While the work was a pleasant surprise, it aligned with the franchise motto "Once a Raider, always a Raider." Even after my fall from grace, Mark Davis embraced me. And once the Raiders' billion-dollar gallery, a gleaming onyx stadium just off the Strip, was complete, the job continued. My paintings of famous musicians such as Frank Sinatra, Sammy Davis Jr., Louis Armstrong, and B. B. King lined the stadium walls.

Johnny Cash.

I'd been away from football for so long by this point that I didn't seriously contemplate a return. I sought some connection to the game that shaped me, though. So I became a volunteer quarterback coach in 2017 for the SoCal Coyotes, a semipro football team in Palm Springs, California.

I worked with Buzzy regularly during this period, leveraging his evolved training protocols. No longer the guinea pig of my youth, my body responded well to his science-based methods. It all paid off when the quarterback abruptly left the team. With no viable backup, I grabbed a helmet after a seventeen-year hiatus. Joining the players on the field, I looked more like their dad than a teammate; however, I had the stamina of a twenty-year-old. My one game was a resounding success. I threw seven touchdowns for a 73–0 victory. Buzzy looked on from the stands in tears. The win didn't matter as much as seeing him happy and proving I could play at forty-eight.

There was one massive problem, though: I lied. Everyone thought I was sober. It was billed as my first game without drugs since age fifteen—not true. I received an injection of painkillers to play through the chronic ache in my shoulder. The moment the drugs hit my system, I was fucked, losing another round in the dogfight to stay clean.

I quit the game forty-eight hours after throwing my last touchdown. Hanging up my helmet forever, I headed to southern Oregon for a vacation with my kids. I didn't want to hear the media weigh in on my abbreviated return to football. Hell no. That's when I smoked a joint, opening the doors to a full-blown relapse. I was so overwhelmed by my spiral that I felt sick, not high. All my faith and hard work went down the drain once again.

Every time I relapsed, I knew the risks—I was playing another round of Russian roulette. They say that relapse is part of the learning process of recovery. Addicts who chronically relapse, however, usually die. Even with that knowledge, I convinced myself it wouldn't happen to me. Then I received a stark reminder. Another one of my good friends, sober for two years, died of a heroin overdose, just like Marco. This should've altered my trajectory, but that presumption would underestimate the power of addiction. Unlike sports, where there was steady progress in lockstep with effort, this disease was unpredictable. Taking another drag in the parking lot while the kids slept, I closed my eyes and hung on for dear life.

I came up with all sorts of reasons for my substance abuse over the years. During my teens, drugs were a social lubricant. They helped me fit in while creating an escape valve for the near-constant internal and external pressure. This was not an excuse but an explanation. I had no way of knowing that this early use would embolden the seeds of disease. The invasive illness sought attachment to something besides football. It found another easy target. When I entered college, my growing addiction fed on regular access to party drugs in an atmosphere of enablement. While substances were often part of college experimentation, they weren't for a budding addict. Drugs were regular irrigation on a poisonous weed. When I reached the NFL, the abuse raged like a forest fire, fed by the flames of fame and fortune. With several million dollars and an out-of-control drug habit, I was able to give addiction its forever home.

Early in recovery, I embraced the role of victim, blaming Marv for everything. He was an easy target. Caught in a cultural flash point where stage moms and dads were criticized for living through their children, he was in the media's crosshairs. One major problem: he didn't fit the role. That didn't stop reporters from lazily relying on surface facts, though. Cheap shots were easy, and sensationalized storylines earned more eyes and ears. I joined the hog pile for a time, as guilty as everyone else. If ESPN called him one of the worst sports fathers ever, why couldn't I? It was convenient but not entirely accurate.

The demon was never Marv; it was always addiction. It was a disease we shared. While mine toggled fluidly from football to drugs, Marv's focused on athletic training. It drove all his actions for sixty-plus years. Did it have consequences? Sure, it left many of Marv's relationships in tatters. As for me, the impact was far more public and even more disastrous. The visible nature of my mistakes and misunderstanding of my illness made everything worse. Rather than compassion, I encountered repulsion. Like many addicts, I represented the inconvenient truth that addiction, once it grabbed hold, was ruthless. No one wanted to face that fact until it was their son, daughter, sister, or uncle.

I prayed that this disease would spare my children.

Coco once asked me about missteps. "Dad, what are mistakes?" She looked up with perfect innocence in her clear, unblinking eyes.

"There are no mistakes, truly none." I paused to let her ponder my response, holding her gaze a little longer, and then pressed on. "A mistake is just something that gets you closer to the person you want to be." I wanted to add something else, but it will come in time. I will beg her to forgive herself when she errs. I don't want her to be half as cruel as I was to myself.

Quality time with my Coco.

Remarkably, I never suffered from depression throughout the highs and lows. Of course, it was devastating to blow up my life, but not in a clinical sense. Instead of depression, I battled something just as sinister: self-sabotaging inner dialogue. My mind was a lethal weapon pointed directly at me, going full throttle in the latter half of 2017. It told me lies and poisoned the good in my life with remarkable success. It took another stint in rehab to see the crazy thoughts for what they were: ugly and hurtful.

Counselors encouraged me to be gentle with myself. That was like telling a boxer not to throw a punch. All I knew was the negative self-talk, which had been as reflexive as breathing since childhood. I couldn't wrap my head around making a change this late in the game. Yet when I spoke my inner dialogue aloud, every member of the group therapy session shuddered.

"I'm a fuckup. Every single time I fail at recovery. It's hopeless," I stated in disgust.

"If a stranger sitting next to you was saying those things, you'd move away," another addict commented after my rant.

I paused, analyzing his words before responding, unsure whether I possessed the terms in my vocabulary to articulate my feelings. "I don't know how to be gentle with myself." I shrugged my shoulders and looked around the room. Everyone in the circle stared back with sadness, reflecting my own. They appeared to be mourning the living.

The facilitator weighed in next. "It comes down to awareness. Be conscious of your thoughts. Recognize how violent your words can be." With a face more beat-up than a catcher's mitt, she clearly spoke from experience.

I nodded, watching the participants do the same.

"If you're that violent toward yourself, how do you think it will translate into your relationships?" she asked, regarding me with eyes that seemed to dissect my heart.

Ouch. She'd nailed it. "Not good," I responded, knowing my relationship with Alix and others needed work.

"Yes, not good at all," she agreed. "It's time to practice kindness toward yourself." She looked around the room, letting her last statement hang in the still air.

A few people jotted down notes, but I fixated on two words: *violence* and *kindness*. I knew a lot about violence on the field. And in all that time, I can't recall being compassionate toward myself. I remember telling Mom in college that I didn't want to be Todd Marinovich. I meant it then and still felt that way over thirty-five years later. That's a very long time to be uncomfortable in your skin. Too long.

The facilitator captured my attention with her next statement. "It's an overused saying, but that doesn't make it less true: 'You can't love anyone else until you love yourself.'"

I squirmed in my chair. I hated that one-liner, maybe because I knew it was accurate. And the reality scared me: I didn't like myself one bit.

"It's time to focus on what you like and amplify the best of yourself through those efforts." The facilitator closed her book and wrapped up the session.

What did I enjoy? Helping others. But I was shy. Reaching out didn't come naturally, so that's where I needed to apply my energy. It was time to get uncomfortable. While my head rattled off every reason not to engage others, the rewards outweighed the risks.

Shortly after that session, a counselor who'd helped me fifteen years prior called out of the blue. He needed help breaking through to a Long Beach Polytechnic High School athlete. This counselor had once pulled me out of the depths of a relapse, so I jumped at the chance to return the favor.

"Can you call this kid, maybe a five-minute FaceTime?"

"I can do better than that," I insisted. "Where is he?"

"With me in downtown Long Beach."

I didn't hesitate. "Okay, give me an hour, and I'll be there." I ignored all the reasons not to go, grabbed a T-shirt, and headed up the 405 Freeway to attempt to make a difference in one life. In reality, it wasn't just one. After a front-row seat to years of wreckage, I finally understood that everyone around an addict pays a high price for the inevitable lies, unfulfilled promises, and misguided actions.

I approached the counselor and kid with care, relaxed but

focused. My contact exited quickly so I could break the stranger barrier. Not surprisingly, the boy was desperate for connection, too, and sports established a common bond within minutes. Plus, I had plenty of street cred with my well-known history of addiction. He knew enough about me to appreciate that I'd seen and experienced it all, defying the odds by staying alive.

We took a walk to loosen up our bodies and minds. Then he let it rip.

"I can't break free," he sheepishly admitted.

"I know that feeling all too well." I placed my arm on his shoulder. "It's worth the fight, though. You have your whole life ahead of you."

He looked away, slowed his gait, and fiddled with his sunglasses. I wasn't getting through. I sounded worse than every counselor who tried that line on me back in the day.

I stopped and stood in the middle of the road to state my case.

"Do you want the real deal?" I asked, deadpan.

That got his attention. He stopped and pivoted toward me. "Yeah."

"Things won't get better unless you do. There's no easy way; that's the god's honest truth." I paused long enough for him to look back at me. "I tried every route, but the only way is through. And it's hard . . . no joke. It's the toughest thing I've done. And that's saying a lot after training with Marv Marinovich."

He smiled, aware of the lore. His wall began to crumble.

"And there's one thing I need you to know and always remember, especially in the dark times: you aren't alone. You're never alone."

I don't know if he took my words to heart or how many other voices and years would be needed for a full breakthrough. I do know that my message came from hard-won experience. For me and countless others, addiction was an isolation illness. I became a recluse, with self-inflicted starvation from the human experience. And in an ironic twist, the more I was alone, the lonelier I felt. The only thing that quieted the pain of isolation was drugs.

I had to break the pattern and couldn't succeed alone. Like a dog coming out of a kill shelter, I needed to get comfortable with greater socialization—I had to work to meet more people halfway. My fresh receptivity opened the door to inevitable questions. The common topics were my USC successes, the short-lived Raiders or arena days, and sometimes my struggles if people were courageous. Once I crossed the chasm between stranger and friend, I was hooked on connection—a far healthier addiction. Come to find out, I loved people. Was I still shy? Sure. It was part of me, but in the shadows, overwhelmed by the light of connection.

But all the bonds in the world wouldn't help until I unpacked my childhood trauma. Was mine worse than anyone else's? It was hard to determine without perspective. In therapy, I learned about performance-based love, which explained the periods of harmony that accompanied success. In contrast, when I didn't rise to my potential, the domestic tension in the Marinovich house was unbearable. However, the intensity of my home life was a double-edged sword. I watched Marv and learned how to give myself entirely, but later I applied this skill to both the good and bad with equal fervor. While Marv was tough on me and everyone else in his life, he was nowhere near as damaging as the reel within my head. But the combination of Marv and my inside job lodged trauma in my body for decades. It festered and caused me to act in ways that weren't in line with my true self. If I didn't dance with the pain, it would destroy me.

Another part of my recovery involved making amends. The list of people I'd wronged was long, but the process was cathartic. In addition to spending time with Larry Smith's family in Arizona, I needed to find Raiders owner Mark Davis.

I was living in Palm Springs in 2017 when a friend in my recovery program mentioned that Mark's favorite restaurant was Mitch's on El Paseo. He came in frequently, always setting up at the sushi bar with a reading light, a newspaper, and his favorite dish.

The next time Mark showed up for dinner, my buddy alerted me. I entered the bar determined not to overthink my words and to speak from the heart. Mark had his head in a newspaper and didn't see me approach. I had pregame butterflies as I pushed through the fear.

"Come here often?" I joked, pulling out a stool and taking a seat.

"No shit, hey, Todd." Mark looked genuinely happy to see me.

"I'm stalking you," I said, only half joking. "I've been waiting for a chance to talk. Is now a good time?"

"Sure, this will be far more interesting than the newspaper." He pushed it aside.

"I want to apologize, Mark, to you and your family, along with the entire Raiders organization."

Now I had his attention as he leaned forward.

"I let you guys down back when I was with the team. You gave me the opportunity of a lifetime, and I ruined it all on my own."

"Honestly, there are no hard feelings." There was genuine sympathy in Mark's eyes.

"I just want you to know how sorry I am," I continued.

He cut in. "All is forgiven and forgotten." His eyes met mine longer this time. "I do have one request, though."

"Yes?"

"Please consider coming to a Raiders reunion. We hold them every year. I know so many guys would love to see you."

"Consider it done."

As we wrapped up our time together, Mark touched my forearm. "You know, I'm proud of you for taking responsibility for your life and illness."

As I walked out of the restaurant that night, I felt lighter. There was nothing more liberating than releasing long-held regret into the painted sky.

One of my final amends came in 2022 at the Raiders reunion. I had a gift for Marcus Allen—a portrait I painted over a decade ago. During the revelry, we found a quiet space where I presented my offering and delivered another long-overdue apology.

"I wasn't honest with you back when we played together. I'm so sorry for that," I explained.

With his soulful eyes, Marcus smiled and responded, "You don't need to apologize. It's all good—water under the bridge."

I nodded, but I regretted not explaining my struggles when we were teammates. I was so scared back then. It was nearly impossible to be honest. But if anyone could've helped, it would've been Marcus.

It took serious balls to get that uncomfortable during the ninth step to recovery. I navigated through some very dark emotions, with every fiber in my being clawing to turn back. But after years of half-hearted effort, I consciously decided to surrender to win. It inspired me to write a song, which I performed live when speaking at a recovery meeting in Florida, where several rehab centers came together.

Surrender 2 Win

Crack rocks, sick thoughts, whiskey shots—you gotta
Smack back, needle tracks, tore back
You gotta
Oxies, LSD, ecstasy
You gotta
Surrender 2 win (2x)
When you're out of all your bright ideas
(I had a million and one of 'em)
When nothing will fill that hole inside
(Mine was as big as the Grand Canyon)
Let go and let God free ya—take them steps to the other side . . .
2, 3, 4
Coke whores, liquor stores, wanting more—
China White, speed pipe, fist fight—you gotta
All sucked up, fucked up, like a dump truck
You gotta—surrender 2 win (2x)
Crack rocks, sick thoughts, whiskey shots—you gotta
Smack back, needle tracks, tore back
You gotta

GHB, PCP, and THC—
You gotta surrender 2 win
Surrender to win

There was something else I needed to surrender to during the winter of 2020: losing Buzzy in the eighth decade of his life. I'd had plenty of time to prepare, but that didn't make it easier. The months leading up to his death were a period of intense reflection. I thought about the early days when he was hell-bent on creating the perfect environment for my growth. He was light-years ahead of his time, recognizing the lies told about food and fitness. His refusal to conform gave me a tremendous advantage.

By my teens, he was demonized, with few recognizing his genius. He'd be misunderstood until society caught up. Yes, everything he did seemed extreme, from his training methods to his expression of love. But I understood his motives better than anyone. He wanted to give his son and other athletes the best.

Like most young adults, I wanted a healthy distance while I was in college and starting my professional life. Marv wasn't a regular fixture during that period. It was probably for the best, as he might have seen through my charade. And once the walls came crumbling down, I distanced myself even further out of shame. It wasn't until my genuine attempts at recovery that I found my way back to him. With the benefit of hindsight, I know the unfiltered truth: Marv "Buzzy" Marinovich was neither a devil nor a god. He was fallible, just like everyone else on this earth.

Leaning over Buzzy during the last hour of his life, I spoke from the heart. "If I had to do it all over again, I'd still choose you."

Buzzy, unable to nod, blinked. I didn't have to say another word. He understood as he passed peacefully to the other side.

Chapter Eleven

Full Circle

Coming off another jail stay in 2019, I knew there was no middle ground and no standing still. I was either walking toward or away from a relapse. I had to focus on my recovery, a daily practice. When I adopted a lifestyle dedicated to healing, I was successful. But when I became complacent, I relapsed. It was that simple.

So I habitually rose before dawn, drove to the beach, and watched the sunrise while expressing gratitude. Then, if the waves beckoned, I indulged, bodysurfing my way to the best natural high on earth. Which part of my morning structure held the keys to sustained recovery? I'd pay big money to know, but I suspect it was less about the activity and more about making space to be mindful of my inner workings. It also helped that I had some transferable skills in my tool kit from decades in football. Discipline, mental fortitude, and grit were equally valuable off the field.

During the day, I poured myself into my art and kids but couldn't shake a nagging feeling that something was missing. I was still searching for a place to heal away from my all-too-well-known existence in Southern California. I was also keenly aware of the growing pressure on my son, Baron. He was an aspiring quarterback growing up with the burden of the Marinovich legacy in Orange County. I needed to protect him from the pressure cooker.

I racked my brain, searching for the right spot to call home. My first thought was Oregon, but it didn't sit right in my head. It wasn't a place I'd stayed sober for long. Then I considered Hawaii, where I lived briefly in the 1970s when Marv coached in the World Football League (WFL). My first recollections were of soft air, endless beaches, and football—not bad memories. But I trusted my gut when I flew into Oahu: it told me to keep looking. The next island was Kauai, associated with a vivid memory from high school when I visited with a friend. Again, something beckoned me further afield. Ready to give up on Hawaii, I took one last flight to the Big Island. I landed in Kona, pulled in a deep, long breath, and knew I was home.

But what would I do so far from life as I knew it? It didn't take long for football to find me, an old love renewed, as I coached teens at the local high school. My addictive personality latched on, but in a positive way this time. I was obsessed with serving these kids. I'd wake up thinking about them and their talents, planning drills, and dreaming about their futures. More than anything, I wanted them to have fun. With plenty of good and bad coaches as my guide, I shaped a program that I am proud of. Would Buzzy have approved? Most definitely, yes. Marv? Not so much. Instead of doing three hours of football and gym work, we practiced for an hour before heading to the beach. And guess what? We still had a great season.

Then I established a flag football program for eight-to-twelve-year-old kids in my community. It brought me back to my first experience with a similar program at age five.

———

When my family moved to Oahu, it didn't take long for Mom to sign me up for flag football.

"Your first practice is tomorrow," she explained, unpacking the last few boxes in my new bedroom.

"What if the other kids don't like me?" I was sprawled out on the floor, still in my Spider-Man pajamas. If I had my way, I'd stay right there playing with a G.I. Joe with my imaginary friend Timmy. My fear of the unfamiliar was acute after the move. For the first time, I didn't look like many of the other kids in class. My red hair, pale skin, and freckles were a walking billboard: I was a *haole*, an insult tossed at non-natives on the islands.

"You will be fine," Mom assured me.

Marv was busy settling into his coaching role in the WFL, so Mom drove me to the first practice. I was all nerves. I approached the amorphous pod of kids with a skyscraper of an adult rattling off instructions.

"You must be Todd," the soft-spoken, gentle-eyed adult said as I approached. "Grab your flags. We're about to get started."

I nodded. They were colorful plastic streamers. The red ones looked enticing. The artist in me couldn't resist a pop of color against my gray shorts.

"Can I be red?" I asked sheepishly.

"You bet, kiddo."

Things were off to a good start. I grabbed my set along with a cloth belt.

Then the self-soothing began. I spent the entire practice stroking my flags. No matter what it took, I wouldn't part with those beautiful streamers. Even mid-run, I'd zealously peer down to ensure they were still affixed. That's all I remember from those early days: my obsession with the flags.

When I became a coach and watched the same performance from my childhood play out before my eyes, I grinned wide. I realized that some behaviors defied space and time as I watched these playful kids in action. Along with having plenty of fun, they learned football fundamentals without the big hits. I felt it was my duty to protect them during these early years. For kids without fully developed brains, tackle football was just plain dangerous. And helmets only offered a false sense of security. After losing so many teammates to CTE, I wasn't about to let any of those kids follow suit—and that included Baron. I'd been heavy-handed about very few things over the years, but this was one. He never stopped begging, but I stood my ground.

"Everyone else is playing tackle football, Dad," he insisted at age nine.

"Not until high school, Baron," I reminded him. "How about basketball, baseball, or golf?" I prayed distraction might solve the problem.

"Can't wait that long," he shot back, dismissing my attempts to divert his interest.

"But you will." I stood firm. "You have to trust me on this one."

"But what if I fall behind?"

"I won't let that happen. Lucky for you, I know a bit about playing quarterback."

Baron rolled his eyes and finished his waffle, drowning in a puddle of syrup—no shamrock shake in sight. I did plenty of things differently than Marv, showing my devotion in other ways, but both versions were love just the same.

Then, when I thought there wasn't room for more love in my heart, Annie entered my life. It all started rather innocently when I launched a flag football league in the remote town of Naalehu, Hawaii. I drummed up a fair bit of interest, chatting with parents and plastering the town with flyers. One of those ads made its way into her hands.

Apparently, she balked at the chutzpah of a mainlander showing up on the island thinking he knew what was best for its kids. But her friend persisted, suggesting that despite my bold move, I seemed like a decent guy with good intentions.

She finally buckled, sending her father and children to the opening day in July 2022.

I fell in love with her kids immediately. Then they showed up with their mom in tow at the next practice. I stopped mid-instruction when I caught her approach in my peripheral vision.

She moved with the grace of a distance runner, her fluid gait designed to maximize output. Within ten yards, I realized she was not only an athlete but an effortless beauty with soulful eyes and kindness that radiated from her generous smile. It felt like divine intervention when our worlds collided.

"I'm Todd," I offered, holding out my hand even though I was dying to hug her. I wanted to know if this crazy chemistry was real or imagined.

"Annie," she replied, with a hint of skepticism despite the smile.

"Your kids are great. Thanks for bringing them," I said as they scattered to link up with their friends.

"We're just trying this out," she cautioned. I read between the lines: she wasn't all in on flag football or "team Todd" for that matter.

"My priority is keeping them safe." I failed to mention a new close second: getting to know their equally remarkable mother.

After our initial meeting, she warmed up quickly while her two sons fell in love with flag football. As for that line "When you know, you know," well, it was true in my case. I intrinsically knew Annie and her kids would be an important part of my journey. It didn't take long for Baron and me to join their clan.

Baron, well versed in the role of older brother, opened his arms to Annie's young children. But he also had plenty to distract him. To no one's surprise, guess who played varsity football his freshman year, starting at quarterback? Yes, history repeated itself despite my best attempts to divert him.

I prayed that our common interests wouldn't also include drugs, which were rampant on the island. With fentanyl on the rise, there was plenty to keep me edgy, not only for myself but for my kids. Luckily for me, my prayers were answered. But if someone was on the road toward destruction, I knew what they needed: love. The best way was to love them right through it like Mom and Buzzy did for me. As Bob Marley said, "Overcome the devils with a thing called love."

I also knew what didn't work: punishment. Well over a century ago, the United States made drugs illegal and forced offenders into a criminal justice system. It was never designed to address addiction. Instead of attending to the underlying causes, the system put barriers in place, such as criminal records limiting an addict's ability to reconnect with the world productively.

How has that worked out? Not well by any measure. Over 85 percent of prisoners suffer from addiction or are jailed for crimes related to drugs. Meanwhile, overdose deaths exceeded one hundred thousand in 2023, with strong links between feelings of isolation and substance abuse.

I'm no expert on reform, but I know there are other options. In 2001, Portugal decriminalized drugs for personal use in an attempt to rescue its population from an overwhelming problem, the worst in Europe at the time. This freed up resources formerly used to isolate addicts, allowing the country to instead use the funds to help addicts reconnect with their communities through work, purpose, and social relationships. The nation even created jobs and offered microloans for recovering substance abusers. While this would be a radical departure from our current system, it could save lives and create an environment of inclusion where we see people like me for more than just our disease.

Looking past my illness, many questions lingered from outside and within. *Was I meant to do what I was good at? Or did this lead to my demise?* After much reflection, I know with absolute certainty that I wasn't put on earth to throw spirals. That's why I felt empty when hitting the top of my game. Football was a part of my journey, but it was far from the most significant phase. I believe with all my heart that I was put here to connect—to reach people who suffer by sharing my experience.

In football, theory was fundamental, but observing other players offered more than any clipboard diagram. Learning about the challenges teammates and role models faced inspired me to persevere and weather occasional setbacks. While I'm far from an example to emulate, my actions throughout recovery reveal something invaluable for those who struggle: I never give up, no matter how hard or far I fall.

And if you are left wondering if I will remain sober, welcome to the club. What I do know with absolute certainty is that physical sobriety is merely a prerequisite to my current trajectory. Unlike in past attempts, there are more unrelenting requirements now, including sustained self-examination, honesty, and humility. Admitting that I don't know how to live is genuine and incredibly humbling. But it opens me to growth. My experiences with Marv and in football reinforce that there are no shortcuts or substitutes for putting in the time to progress.

Harnessing lessons learned through sports, art, and recovery gives me a fighting chance. It's never too late to become the person I aspire to be despite the past. Living in my truth is a liberation from my history and a freedom unlike anything I've ever known. I wish this sovereignty for everyone on a similar journey.

Epilogue: Hard-Won Wisdom

> How are we supposed to treat others? There are no others.
> —Ramana Maharshi

In my forty years of battling addiction, I've been shamed, demeaned, isolated, and punished for my disease. I am an "other" by society's cruel yardstick. But what if there are no others, as Ramana Maharshi suggests? With one in four people suffering from some form of addiction, are we really comfortable ostracizing on such a grand scale?

Addiction isn't a lack of willpower or a weak state of being. It's an illness, a disease of the brain that varies on a vast spectrum. This adds to the mystery and subsequent confusion about treatment. While it only takes thirty days to reset reward pathways, that doesn't account for chronic users with altered dopamine thresholds that aren't a quick fix.

It certainly hasn't been an easy process for me. When asked

how I feel these days, I remind myself that feelings come and go. My commitment to connection, healing, and a passion for life grounds me. I must show up daily, as consistently as sunrise, for the people I love. They can maneuver around me to make their mistakes, but I will always be there, despite or maybe because of my missteps.

I have taken back my power by sharing my truth. I'm no longer hiding or fighting to escape. I'm a man shaped by glory and suffering with the scars of a loving warrior. The struggle to maintain sobriety is real and consuming, but so is my gratitude as a survivor.

I look back on the self-medicated and anxious young football player who couldn't imagine anyone wanting to be Todd Marinovich in that fateful *Mark & Brian Show* poll back in 1993. Over thirty years later, after much growth and self-reflection, I'd react differently to that poll. I'd nod with a well-worn smile and laughter fueled by the simple joy of being alive.

Acknowledgments

This was a challenging book for me to write. While there were many joyful memories, I ventured down some very dark holes to unearth painful moments too. You deserve to have it all—the good, the bad, and the ugly—from me, not some sportswriter with an agenda or talking head on their soapbox.

They say timing is everything, and that's certainly true of this book. I was settled into a blissful existence in Hawaii when an old Raiders teammate, Steve Wright, reached out to check on me. He told me about his writing journey and encouraged me to pen my memoir. At first, I brushed it off. So many friends over the years have told me my life story should be a book or movie, but I was never in the right emotional space to tackle such a daunting endeavor. However, the seed Steve planted grew this time, slowly, as I sat with the idea. By our next conversation, my mind was open to the undertaking.

Lucky for me, Steve's partner in crime, Lizzy Wright, was available to help bring my story to life. Over nine months, we met weekly to examine events that shaped me, often reliving those moments to deliver you into the passenger seat. My story was far from linear, and Lizzy's analytical mind fluidly navigated the rough road. She was patient with me, intuitively understanding the need to go slowly at times and tread gently at others. I'm grateful for her sensitivity and steady, skillful hand throughout this process. Guided by Lizzy; my agent, Joe Perry; my publisher, Matt Holt; and his amazing team, this work came to life.

While it may seem strange to thank a place, it's not for me. Hawaii has been a dream come true, bringing me tranquility and the space to heal. It offered a new relationship with my children and football and opened my heart to a new future. I wouldn't be the man I am today without its imprint on my life.

My family, who rode my roller coaster so many times, was also steadfast in their support for my recovery, art, writing, and life in Hawaii. Trudi, Traci, Baron, and Coco are my rocks. They continue to love me without condition, and I am forever thankful.

And special thanks to my Trojan and Raiders families for access to the photography archives so that you could not only read about my life but see it throughout all its twists and turns. Finally, to my teammates and friends who supported me in significant and subtle ways during trying times, please know that I will never forget and always carry my love for each of you.

About the Authors

Todd Marinovich was a football media sensation for the last quarter of the twentieth century. In high school, he was the top player in the nation. He was also the star quarterback at the University of Southern California, leading the Trojans to a Rose Bowl victory his freshman year. Selected in the first round of the NFL draft as the first sophomore in history to declare, he joined the Los Angeles Raiders, playing from 1991 to 1993.

Leaving football due to drug addiction, he returned to the sport in 1999, earning Arena Football League All-Rookie team honors in 2000. A widely viewed ESPN Films documentary, *The Marinovich Project*, explored Todd's unconventional life and rise to prominence.

A man who brings lightness and humor to even the most

difficult trials in life, Todd openly shares his story to inspire others. He encourages audiences to embrace their truth, live out loud unapologetically, and pick themselves back up after inevitable falls. A father, coach, and spiritual survivor, Todd resides in Hawaii.

Lizzy Wright's life has been about taking risks and defying the odds. After decades of driving transformation for businesses and nonprofits, she followed her heart into the enchanting world of storytelling. Her education at Harvard and Georgetown and careers in intelligence and consulting honed a distinct analytical eye that enriches Lizzy's writing.

Her first memoir, penned for Steve Wright, *Aggressively Human*, tackles the uneasy intersection between aggression and empathy. In a world where masculinity is a moving target, it exposes a deeply personal quest to become a healthy, well-adjusted man and a fully realized human being.

A lifelong athlete and adventurer, the ocean is Lizzy's second home, where she contemplates character development and word choice in the surf lineup. She lives her dream with her husband, former NFL athlete Steve Wright, in a laid-back enclave of Malibu, California.